CW00933191

# The Book of the
# PATRIOT 4-6-0s

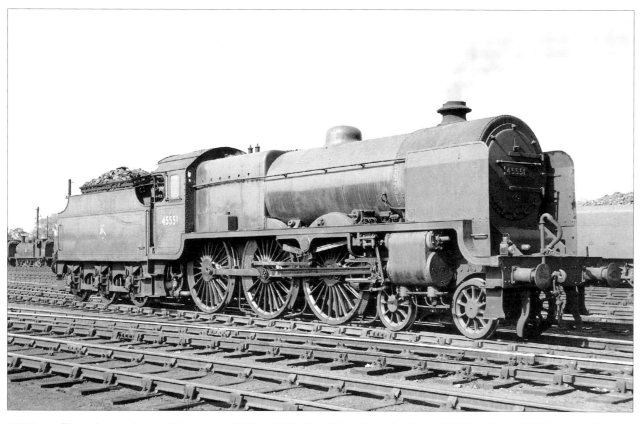

45551, an Upperby engine at Kingmoor, 25 May 1952. The Baby Scots had the old Claughton LNW 'mangle handle' reverser, high up in the cab with a dropped area between driver's and fireman's foot rests – these were in effect the rear wheel splashers. Photograph J. Robertson, The Transport Treasury.

# A British Railways Illustrated Special
## by
## Ian Sixsmith

Copyright IRWELL PRESS LIMITED
ISBN 1-903266-40-8

# Acknowledgements

From *The Book of the Jubilee 4-6-0s*: 'Little that is *wholly* new remains to be said concerning any major class of British steam locomotive, though of course there is still a lot to celebrate and illustrate'. The same point was made in the preceding books of this series – *The Book of the BR Standards*, *The Book of the Coronation Pacifics*, *The Book of the Royal Scots*, *The Book of the Princess Royal Pacifics*, *The Book of the Merchant Navy Pacifics*, *The Book of the West Country and Battle of Britain Pacifics* and *The Book of the BR Standards: 2*. Yet there are always a few nuggets to be had, and this is true I hope in the story of the Patriots. A great part of the photographs have not been seen before and for this special thanks go to Barry Hoper, proprietor of the Transport Treasury. There is more to preservation in railways than you'd think and the saving of its myriad photographic images is one vital facet. Don't let your precious negatives get lost or, worse, get broken up into anonymous lots and disposed of by auctioneers upon your passing. Contact The Transport Treasury: *GATE HOUSE, NORTH ROAD, INSCH, ABERDEENSHIRE, AB52 6XP, 01464 820863.*

Thanks also go to Allan Baker, Hamish Stevenson, Alec Swain, Chris Hawikins, Martin Smith, Geoff Goslin, Eric Youldon, Peter Groom, David Clarke, John Welsh and Peter Rowledge. My thanks above all to Graham Onley, who pursued the diabolical task of checking and re-checking the Tables.

Copies of the original Record Cards, together with some carefully tabulated material, came through the good offices of John Jennison of *Brassmasters*. This cottage manufactory produces high quality kits (not least among the range is the superb 4mm Patriot) in etched brass and other mysterious materials, largely for the love of it. These purveyors of the finest brassware known to Man (who put a *tipping driver's seat* into a 4mm Jubilee and for all I know transmute base metal into gold in their spare time) will be happy to supply lists of their products, details and so on (SEND AN SAE): *BRASSMASTERS SCALE MODELS, PO BOX 1137, SUTTON COLDFIELD, WEST MIDLANDS B76 1FU*; try them also on the web at www.brassmasters.co.uk.

First published in the United Kingdom in 2003
by Irwell Press Limited, 59A, High Street, Clophill,
Bedfordshire MK45 4BE
Printed by Newton Printing

# Contents

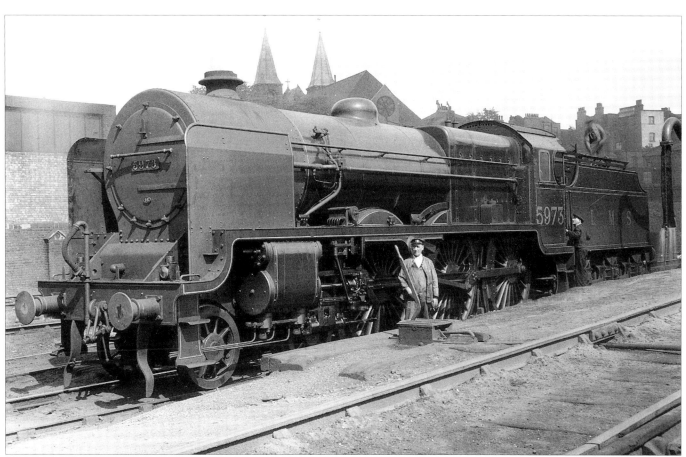

5973 (later 5522) in the early 1930s. It has a 'beaded' tender but in fact both 'beaded' and 'non-beaded' had a topping 'lip' finishing off the tender sides – the eye of faith is needed to distinguish them. 'Beaded' really means 'more beaded than the non-beaded'. It's a question of getting your eye in and it has more importance for some students of Patriots than others. If you're modelling one, at any sort of rational viewing distance, it's hardly something that would be noticed. But there's nothing like donning the hair shirt... compare with say, 5520 on page 13. Photograph The Transport Treasury.

The original Baby Scot, 5971 at Bingley, between Leeds and Skipton, in its early days on the Midland Division. There is a lot of evidence to the effect that the first two Baby Scots had Claughton frames; certainly they had the LNW wheel spacing. They also had the short wheelbase LNW swing link bogie, while the original wheels were re-set on new axles. This was because the LNW used left-hand crank leading. Midland, and hence LMS, practice, was right-hand lead. The original, 5971, spent its first year or so at Holbeck – this was a time, it should be remembered, when the Midland lines, apart from Claughtons drafted in, were still mostly in the hands of Compounds and 2Ps. So often the Aunt Sally, a fleet of twenty or so Baby Scots in the early 1930s, even though their stay was brief, must have bolstered matters a good bit. From 1934/35 of course, increasing numbers of Jubilees were available, and it was decided to concentrate the Baby Scots on the Western Division. 'Patriots' did not appear officially until 1937 and to the end, on the working railway, they were called Baby Scots. In the first picture, 5971, running curiously with a blank plate before the name CROXTETH was applied, is on the down afternoon London-Glasgow (note LNER coaches for Edinburgh at the front); in the second the train is the up Thames-Clyde. Whatever you say, and though the LNW had used the name proudly in days of yore, a Liverpool suburb, whatever its undoubted merits, was hardly fit for the 'first of the class'. Could we have ended up with the 'Suburb' 4-6-0s, with jewels such as 'South Wembley'? Photographs courtesy Geoff Goslin, The Gresley Society.

# A Rose By Any Other Name...
## 'Claughtons', 'Baby Scots', 'Patriots' and 'Taper Scots'

It is generally appreciated and understood that LMS motive power affairs had experienced something of a nadir by the early 1930s. At the risk of reducing the complex story to something fairy tale-like, William Stanier then appeared and, with his 'mighty re-stocking', saved the day. Many written accounts attest to this, not least earlier efforts in this series such as *The Book of the Coronation Pacifics*, *The Book of the Royal Scots*, *The Book of the Princess Royal Pacifics* and *The Book of the Jubilee 4-6-0s*.

Yet before Stanier's arrival from the GWR on 1 January 1932 some significant developments had taken place; Stanier's Jubilees became the LMS 'Second Division' engines but such a second ranking, or 5X class of locomotive, had first sidled onto the LMS stage in the shape of twenty modified Claughton 4-6-0s, introduced from 1928. These had been fitted with new (Derby-designed) 'G9½S' boilers and ten of them got Caprotti valve gear. Nevertheless this was never exactly going to revolutionise matters and these larger boiler Claughtons hardly starred in any sort of role as 'the Second Division after the Royal Scots.

The Claughtons had been an obvious choice, for despite their obsolescent looks they were fairly new, the last having been completed as late as 1921. With the bigger boiler they were, however, superior in power to the rest of the Claughtons and they were designated 5X instead of 5. Indicating a power capability some way between the 5 of the Claughtons generally and the 6 of the Royal Scots, it seems to have been the first use of the designation.

This then was the origin of the 'Second Division' eventually occupied very largely by the Jubilees. Yet clearly something better than enlarged Claughtons, with their weak chassis and poor repair record would be necessary. In 1930, then, the LMS decided on a much more extensive 'rebuilding', this time of two Claughtons. The relevant Locomotive Committee minute, of 23 October 1930, speaks of 'alterations' to two Claughtons, estimated at £1,850 each plus £600 for patterns. The term 'alterations' was necessary for accounting purposes for they were, self-evidently, largely 'new' engines. The Locomotive Committee noted that the new engines were to utilise new frames, spare tenders and 'existing boilers'. The latter, it must be stressed, meant an *existing type*. It did not necessarily mean a second-hand boiler,

though the two used, No.5363 and No.5365, were actually a couple of years old – they would have been the next two overhauled examples available. Whereas the Claughton was a four cylinder machine, the resultant conversion had, like a Royal Scot, three cylinders.

The two engines to emerge from Derby with the new enlarged 'G9½S' boiler as fitted to the twenty upgraded Claughtons were 5971 and 5902, in November 1930. These were the first Patriots, though the term was still some time in the future. From their appearance, the timing of their introduction and their secondary roles, they were, of course, the 'Baby Scots', classified 5XP. Another forty were to be 'rebuilt' from Claughtons. A Locomotive Committee minute of January 1932 declared these later engines to be 'complete renewals' even though Engine History cards mistakenly note them as 'converted from ordinary Claughtons'. A price of some £5,100 was certainly about right for a new engine at this time – the 'conversion' of the first two, in which the term was more appropriate it will be recalled (see above) was under £2,000.

Tests in the meantime with the first two 'Baby Scots' had been

A Baby Scot in early condition on the West Coast route. 5987 (later 5504, later still ROYAL SIGNALS) went straight to the Western Division but did find itself on the Midland lines much later on, as part of the final Patriot allocation to Bristol Barrow Road. With the first type of straight deflector, it is passing Bletchley with the up Merseyside Express. Fire bell and sign prominent on station building. Photograph courtesy Geoff Goslin, The Gresley Society.

Baby Scot and Royal Scot on the ash pits at what looks to be Camden. 5507 ROYAL TANK CORPS was named at the end of 1937 and was at 3A Bescot from September 1937 to March 1939, so this is the period we're looking at. The Scot behind is 6108 SEAFORTH HIGHLANDER. Note the trolleys on rails alongside and within the pit, for ash/clinker removed via firehole door and cab. Photograph H.C. Doyle, courtesy Geoff Goslin, The Gresley Society.

encouraging. 5971 had gone to the Midland Division, at Holbeck, and 5902 went to Crewe, on the Western Division, so their abilities on a wide range of work – especially hill climbing north of Leeds and Crewe – could be established. In February 1931 the second of the two Baby Scots, 5902, had been run in comparison with re-boilered Claughtons; a Caprotti one, 5908, and a 'standard' one, 5910, both with valve gear specially honed for the occasion. The test ground was Euston-Manchester, with ordinary service trains, and while nothing striking seems to have emerged, the Baby Scot proved better on coal consumption. The Patriot, it is safe to say, was a very

The second Baby Scot and the first to bear a (subsequently changed) name, 5902 SIR FRANK REE. Note steam sanding.

Ungainly progenitor – large boiler Claughton 5948 BALTIC (one of the ones to get Caprotti valve gear) at Bletchley in the 1930s. Photograph Dr Ian C. Allen, The Transport Treasury.

good engine – a darn sight better, in fact, than the earlier Jubilees when they were experiencing temperamental steaming.

The first two Baby Scots and the subsequent forty 'conversions' built 1932-1933 kept, presumably for appearances, the numbers of the Claughtons they 'replaced' though it is fascinating that in the case of the first two and the first batch, from Crewe, of 1932, the condemnation dates of the Claughtons and the dates to traffic of their 'conversions' are the same. For the twenty-five subsequently 'converted' and put into service in 1933 the condemnation dates are two-three months earlier. Logical of course, but we engine-pickers delight in these unexplained differences. *Why*, we wonder.

With the forty Baby Scots built over 1932-1933, there came a final ten built unashamedly 'new' These came in 1934 and took new numbers straight away – 5542-5551. It would appear that ten of Lot 95 might have been transferred to Crewe from Derby at an early date:

The final ten, 5542-5551, had been allocated numbers at the end of the Claughton series, 6030-6039 (remember the Baby Scots had numbers scattered throughout the Claughtons) but the new tidy ordering of 1934 saw them placed at the end of the renumbered Baby Scots instead. The original 'Claughton' numbers of the first forty-two are as follows:

| | |
|---|---|
| 5971 (5500) | 5933 (5521) |
| 5902 (5501) | 5973 (5522) |
| 5959 (5502) | 6026 (5523) |
| 5985 (5503) | 5907 (5524) |
| 5987 (5504) | 5916 (5525) |
| 5949 (5505) | 5963 (5526) |
| 5974 (5506) | 5944 (5527) |
| 5936 (5507) | 5996 (5528) |
| 6010 (5508) | 5926 (5529) |
| 6005 (5509) | 6022 (5530) |
| 6012 (5510) | 6027 (5531) |
| 5942 (5511) | 6011 (5532) |
| 5966 (5512) | 5905 (5533) |
| 5958 (5513) | 5935 (5534) |
| 5983 (5514) | 5997 (5535) |
| 5992 (5515) | 6018 (5536) |
| 5982 (5516) | 6015 (5537) |

| | |
|---|---|
| 5952 (5517) | 6000 (5538) |
| 6006 (5518) | 5925 (5539) |
| 6008 (5519) | 5901 (5540) |
| 5954 (5520) | 5903 (5541) |

## PATRIOT

The name PATRIOT, borne so famously in turn by two Claughtons (2097 from April 1917 until January 1920 and 1914 new from January 1920 until withdrawn as LMS 5991 in 1935) was in danger of lapsing out of use and, after some public and private urgings, the LMS decided it should indeed be perpetuated, on 5500. The locomotive was duly named in 1937, allowing the class to be dubbed 'the Patriots'. This was not at all to the liking of O.S. Nock and I must say it is hard to disagree with him. The significance and symbolism of the second PATRIOT (numbered 1914 and in black) had already been diluted through its renumbering and painting in red by the time it had been withdrawn in 1935 and Nock seems to suspect the move had more to do with getting rid of the term 'Baby Scot'. Nock regarded the deep and sombre import of the name as unsuited to a whole class of engines, especially as a number had nondescript names or no names at all. Mind you, as an old boy, he seemed to approve of GIGGLESWICK! In any event, from 1937 on the term 'Patriots' is properly applicable, though many never stopped using 'Baby Scot'.

| Built | Lot No. | 1934 Nos. | Works | Order No. |
|---|---|---|---|---|
| 1930 | 74 | 5500/1 | Derby | 7560 |
| 1932 | 87 | 5502-11 | Crewe | X934 (boilers B369) |
| | 88 | 5512-6 | Crewe | X33 (boilers B370) |
| 1933 | 95 | 5517-9/23/4 | Crewe | X33 (boilers B370) |
| | | 5529-32/6-41 | Crewe | 379 |
| 1934 | 96 | 5542-51 | Crewe | 380 |
| 1934 | 98 | 5520-2/5-8/33-5 | Derby | 8179 |

The ancient Claughton wheel centres, on PATRIOT at Willesden, 11 January 1959. Photograph Peter Groom.

## Conversion

Thinking ahead to the power requirements on the post-war LMS, it was envisaged that all the 'Second Division', that is the Patriots and Jubilees, together with the parallel boiler Royal Scots, would be converted to 6P (later 7P under BR) taper boiler form, something along the lines of the rebuilt experimental high pressure FURY, as BRITISH LEGION. This would have yielded a truly staggering stock of express engines and after BRITISH LEGION the real forerunners were two Jubilees, 5735 COMET and 5736 PHOENIX – as is closely related in *The Book of the Jubilee 4-6-0s*. As is recounted there, the odd thing, as it turned out, was that while all the Royal Scots and many of the Patriots would be converted, COMET and PHEONIX would be the only Jubilees to get 2A taper boilers. The LMS authorised eighteen Patriots

for rebuilding as part of its post-war '6P' plans, a programme that was to be completed by BR. With new BR Standard designs on the horizon (in particular the Clan Pacifics) no further conversions were authorised and, as *The Book of the Jubilees* puts it, 'that was that'.

The two Jubilees appeared with new 2A boilers and double exhaust, in April and May 1942, a month or so before the first ten Royal Scot conversions were authorised. The new-style Jubilees performed well working out of Holbeck, sufficient to ensure the authorisation of further Royal Scot conversions. In 1945 the Patriots were drawn into the programme, Job No. 5390 issued in August 1945 declaring: *'To meet post war needs of accelerated express passenger services it has been decided to convert eighteen 5X parallel engines to take taper boilers; eight boilers in 1946 Programme.*

*Engines to be selected when requiring boiler overhaul. To have 4,000 gallon tenders'.*

Eighteen were duly transformed with the 2A taper boilers – the work, again, went far beyond 'rebuilding' and again, the Accountant must have been responsible for the classification. The work was described in the Crewe notes as being 'converted to Taper Scot' and over a couple of years or so from 1946 the Patriots were indeed 'converted to Taper Scots' in a very similar form indeed to the new Royal Scots. A minor difference was that new Stanier style cabs were fitted to the Patriots. (The original Patriot cab was too narrow.)

All the 'new' Patriots were ordered to have self-cleaning smokeboxes and while the first eight, it is said, got only new front ends to the frames, the rest, the other ten, had completely new frames incorporating the most recent improvements to design standards, materials and construction. There is, however, a 'dissenting point' to be made here – what might be called 'Baker's Theorem' after its progenitor, Allan C. Baker, who started his long professional career at Crewe North. One significant difference between the two taper converted Jubilees, 5735-5736, lay in the front guardirons or 'lifeguards'. The rebuilt Jubilees had the lifeguard mounted on the bogie frames, angled out towards the rails; all Jubilees had this Swindon-style arrangement from new, even the short firebox engines. The rebuilt Scots/ Patriots had the 'Derby' style – these were downward extensions of the main frame, as had been the case prior to rebuilding. So it would seem, on the face of it, that even when rebuilt, the Patriots *retained* the original frames (or at least ones of exactly the same design) as did the Scots. Along with the Scots, the 2A Patriots got new frames *before* rebuilding – otherwise why not 'Stanierise' the mainframes? Much easier to repair a damaged lifeguard! It was strange, as all the engines except the original Patriots eventually had the Churchward design of Stanier bogie.

The choice of the eighteen Patriots to be rebuilt was not haphazard; the engines were done as they became due for boiler renewal, as the Locomotive Committee quote reveals. It has been said that the first twelve 'Baby Scots' 5500-5511 were, for one non-standard reason or another, not suitable for conversion, though a (wishful?) 1950 BR memorandum (see *Clans?* below) contradicts this. The real reason would appear to lie in the varied wheelbases revealed next under the heading *Some Patriot Dimensions*. Whatever, after the eighteenth Patriot, conversion work stopped except for the Royal Scots (they were not complete until 1955) and COMET and PHOENIX remained the only '6Ps' among the Jubilees. All

6018 PRIVATE W. WOOD, V.C. under construction at Crewe in 1933. The RCTS volume relating to LMS names tells us that the original LNW nameplate did not have the comma after the Private's name. 6018 became 5536 in 1934.

the 2A boilered engines, Scots, Patriots and the two Jubilees, became 7P from 1951 under the BR power classification scheme.

**Some Patriot Figures/Dimensions**
*Cylinders (original) 18in x 26(3)*
*Cylinders (rebuilt) 17in x 26in (3)*
*Working pressure (original) 200psi*
*Working pressure (rebuilt) 250psi*
*Tractive Effort @85% (original) 26,520lb*
*Tractive Effort @85% (rebuilt) 29,590lb*
*Coupled wheelbase*
*7ft 4in plus 8ft 0in (7ft 5in plus 7ft 10in for 5500/1)*
*Coupled wheels*
*6ft 9in diameter*
*Bogie wheelbase*
*6ft 3in (5500-5511)*
*6ft 6in (5512-5551)*
*Bogie wheels*
*3ft 3in diameter*
*Tender wheels*
*4ft 3in diameter*
*Total wheelbase varied...*
*5500/5501 = 29ft 0in*
*5502-5511 = 27ft 5½in*
*5512-5551 = 27ft 7in*
*So we have three wheelbases whereas up to now most of us knew only of one! The first two had the Claughton wheelbase, as described when new in* The Railway Gazette. *This also gives the reason for excluding 5500-5511 when fitting the 2A boiler because of the bogie type. The LMS always quoted the second! See also the preceding section* Conversion.

**DETAILS, DETAILS**
The story, overall, of the Patriots, is mercifully short, especially compared with the Jubilees, say, or the Royal Scots even though, like those other two classes, they managed to get built into two wholly different forms. The 'engine-picking' side of things is relatively straightforward, for a change. As the purveyors of the *Brassmasters* exquisite 4mm kits of these wonderful locomotives put it, *'the visual differences were mainly subtle and require close study to identify them on photographs, and most were in common with those applied to the other standard LMS classes.'* Yet there is enough detail variation among the two completely different types, 'Baby Scot' and 'Taper Scot' to satisfy the most devoted engine-picker. I hope to be able to list some of the more important ones here – one, long unsuspected, was the difference in bogie wheelbase, just as with the Jubilees. This has the status of 'breaking news', at least to some of us.

**Wheels**
The first two, 5971 and 5902 (5500, 5501) came out from Derby with the LNWR Claughton pattern wheels; these had a distinctive profile and enormous central bosses. Subsequent batches had LMS pattern wheels; in these, the space between the two spokes projecting from the crank were filled with a sheet of metal. The last batch had Stanier wheels, according to

the study notes produced by *Brassmasters*. These had triangular section rims with the filled space spanning the three spokes on either side of the cranks. Wheels moved around between locomotives and even between Royal Scots, Jubilees and Patriots and some photographs show a mix of types on the same locomotive. More importantly, there was the curious 'webbing' first described and illustrated in *The Book of the Jubilee 4-6-0s* page 22.

Earlier Fowler wheels, especially on the Royal Scots, suffered tyre fracture failures, approaching twenty a year at one time on the LMS. That's the *total* failures, not per loco! By the time Stanier arrived, the LMS had established the more robust 'V' or bevelled rim which virtually eliminated tyre failures. A 'Gibson' ring – named after its American inventor – kept rims in place should they become loose. From about this time the 'filled-in' space/spaces between the spokes radiating out from the crankpin seem to have given way to the 'webbing' already mentioned. This was applied to the four short spokes closest to the crankpin, which were still relatively vulnerable to failure despite the wheel improvements – if they did not have the reinforced 'webbing' that is. Most of these 'subtle' variations, as *Brassmasters* so rightly describe them, can be teased out of photographs if you are lucky with the light. The 'webbing', once again, could be found variously

5916 E. TOOTAL BROADHURST at Kentish Town shed in May 1934. It had appeared the previous year and within a couple of months would become 5525. Until E. TOOTAL BROADHURST appeared, along with 5907 SIR FREDERICK HARRISON, only one Baby Scot (the second one, 5902 SIR FRANK REE) bore a name – you need the RCTS *LMS Locomotive Names* to sort out this specialised subject. The name E. TOOTAL BROADHURST was in any event removed, early in 1937, and given to 5534, 5525 running nameless for a while – perhaps only a few months – until it was named COLWYN BAY. There are some more instances like this, unfortunately. To return to the stirring portrait of 5916; the loco is standing alongside the distinctive bottling stores at Kentish Town, which provided an almost ecclesiastical background. Note the three sanders – already steam by now – and the filler lids, 'knobbed' type with supporting brackets. The cab has yet to get the rain strip which altered the appearance so. Long cylinder drain pipes, clipped to rear of front steps. Photograph A.G. Ellis, The Transport Treasury.

distributed both among individual locos and between the three main LM passenger 4-6-0 classes.

## Cabs

The *look* of the cabs on the original engines, the Baby Scots, changed greatly, though the modification was tiny. As first built, the cab side met the roof with an apparently seamless curve. Well, not so much curve, more a change of direction. It was the sort of look typified in say, the later GW pannier tank cabs. The addition of a rain strip from about 1935 changed the appearance completely. Less obvious was the fitting of a vertical glass wind deflector strip. On such foundations is the great edifice of engine-picking constructed. The cabs on the original two, 5971 and 5902 (5500, 5501) were different from the later production batches, for the side sheets had flush riveting instead of the snap head rivets of the later locomotives.

## Coupling Rods

The Patriots had plain coupling rods but of course the first two were different – 45500 and 45501 had fluted rods, apparently right to the end of their lives.

## Cylinders

The first Baby Scots, up to 5983 (5514) at any rate, had 'enclosed' cylinder draincocks. In actual fact they were not 'enclosed' – this is a convenient way of describing them. They were combined cylinder drain cocks and pressure relief valves – a Midland design which altered in detail later on on the original engines. The 2A conversions had the Stanier arrangement of separate cylinder covers, one on the front cover at the bottom (clearly seen in photographs) and the rear one offset to the outside, to clear the slidebar mounting – less clearly seen in photographs. Cylinder wrappers were plain but after the Second World War a number got small circular cylinder inspection covers with a four bolt fixing. These apparently gave access to a connection for a cylinder lubrication pipe. Cylinder drain cock pipes originally ran right to the front, by the look of it being clipped to the rear of the footsteps. Later these were severely cut back.

## Crosshead-driven Vacuum Pump

The left-hand slidebars of the Patriots carried prominent vacuum pumps, just as the Royal Scots and the Jubilees did at first. Their purpose was to maintain enough vacuum to keep the brakes off when the engine was coasting. It was eventually perceived that a small ejector could do the work just as efficiently, without the nuisance of keeping the pumps maintained and from the late 1930s all were removed. There had long been even darker doubts concerning the pumps and the Aucterarder accident to a Scot on an overnight Perth in 1936 was the worst of several failures attributed to the undue loading from the pump. The crosshead bracket driving the pump fractured and the little end came adrift. Eventually the rod penetrated the firebox, with disastrous consequences. The Modification for the work, replacement of the vacuum pumps by 'combined ejectors', Job 5088, was finally issued in August 1938.

## Bufferbeams

The front bufferbeams were plain at first but by BR days most had snaphead riveting.

## Names

Many of the names were 'nondescript and quite irrelevant' in the opinion of O.S. Nock (*The Royal Scots and Patriots of the LMS*, D&C, 1978). The military ones and one or two others aside, the names were not really adequate for a class heading of 'Patriot' with all its sombre and reverential war memorial associations. And really, Nock has to be right, though the point was much less obvious to later generations. The names were applied haphazardly and, worse, were swopped about between some examples – a tithe or more had no names at all. There was, it must be said, a certain homeliness to some of the Patriot names – with all respect to the good townsfolk, Rhyl, Bangor, Blackpool and Fleetwood lacked something of the stirring ring enjoyed by the likes of Aboukir, Implacable, Black Watch and the rest.

## Speedos

The Patriots, so far as can be determined, did not get speedometers (or 'speed recorders' as they would have been then) under the LMS. In the early 1960s Stone-Delta speedometers driven off the left-hand trailing crankpin began to appear especially, on the LM, on Jubilees, Royal Scots and Pacifics. The taper boiler Patriots were certainly included, though it is not clear if all eighteen got them – very probably they did. With some original Patriots already withdrawn and the others slated for 'the chop' it was hardly surprising that none got a speedo.

## Smoke Deflectors, Grab Irons

The story follows the Royal Scots, more or less; the first two Baby Scots did not have smoke deflectors originally but the following ten did. These were the original flat deflectors, which were replaced during 1933-1934 by the familiar curved top plates. The rest of the class emerged with this style from new. Two distinct variants appeared, and these do not appear to have changed on individual locomotives – though don't bet on it. Crewe used a wide 'flat' beading on the outer edges while Derby used a narrower 'rounded' beading. 5500, built at Derby, seems to have been an exception, having picked up the Crewe 'flat' beading somewhere along the line.

The rebuilt taper boiler Patriots, of course, got Royal Scot style deflectors after a while. Like the Scots, some had the small grab iron low down at the front of the deflector, others didn't – it seems to have been a modification applied progressively through the 1950s. Presumably all or most of the taper boiler locomotives ended up with it. As repeated endlessly elsewhere, the golden rule if you require absolute detail accuracy for a model (and why not – some cost thousands) is: get a photograph with a date.

The Patriots, apart from the last ten, originally had a short horizontal grab iron on the front running plate above the foot steps. This was moved to the lower part of the deflectors from the mid-1930s.

## Sanding

Was to front and rear of middle driver and front of leading driver on originals. This was the standard arrangement for Royal Scots, Jubilees and other classes. On the original engines there was a prominent square sand box perched on the running plate for the rear supply to the middle driver. The other sandboxes were sited below the running plate, as was normal practice. The lid of the middle sandbox was partly hidden under the reversing shaft, while the front sandbox sat forward of the front splasher. It is very difficult to see on most views, being hidden by the lubricator. The sandbox lids were of various sorts, the Fowler 'domed' ('knobbed' would be a better word) type with or without a supporting bracket or the later Stanier recessed pattern. All seem to have got these recessed handles by the 1940s, and the taper boiler engines got them from new.

While it would seem safe to assume that the original engines had 'dry trickle' (better known as 'gravity') sanding the actual situation is not clear. Look at 5916 in 1934 and the new 5997 at Holbeck for instance, with steam sanding quite evident. From 1938 the Jubilees started getting steam sanding and any Patriots without it would have got it from then too. The converted engines got it from the first, of course.

## Chimneys; Top Feed

There was little variation in the chimneys of the original engines. 6005 (5509) was experimentally fitted with a Kylala exhaust from December 1932, involving a truly awful 'flowerpot' confection of a chimney. In the same tradition, 45508 got a hideous stovepipe in 1956, keeping it till withdrawal. Known as 'the bucket' it was fitted in connection with a draughting experiment. The taper boiler rebuilds had double chimneys from the first.

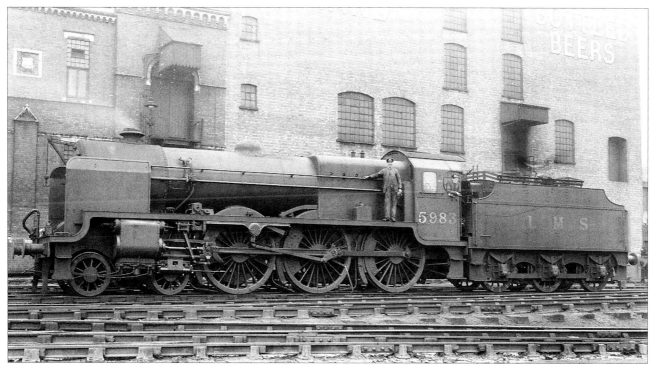

Kentish Town again, with 5983 outside that noble bottling plant. Among its notable products was 'Dog's Head' ale. As 5514 the loco was later named HOLYHEAD, in 1938. Even that was not straightforward – it bore the name only briefly and got it back permanently only in 1947, according to the RCTS. Note middle sand filler lid largely hidden behind reversing lever and vacuum pump driven off left-hand crosshead. It also has the original 'enclosed' cylinder drain cocks (just visible in some other photographs in this book). 5983, built Crewe, has '5X' behind the window; 5916, built Derby, has '5XP', in front of the cab window. Photograph W. Hermiston, The Transport Treasury.

Brand new 5997 at Holbeck on 20 May 1933, positively glowing in the red ('crimson lake') livery of the time and surely brand new. *Steam* sanding. It was named SIR HERBERT WALKER K.C.B, apparently in 1937. The previous owner, 5529 (the preceding Claughton of which had borne the name too) was renamed STEPHENSON in 1948. The great blessing is that the LMS didn't do a lot more of this sort of thing. The curving pipe above the cylinder and behind the smoke deflector is the vacuum connection from the crosshead pump to the train pipe. Photograph The Transport Treasury.

Another short-lived experiment was a curiously exaggerated top feed 'for the right-hand injector' on 5535. This lasted from late 1936 to March 1938. So far as the 'general run' of top feeds went, matters were straightforward enough so far as the original Patriots were concerned – they did not have a top feed ahead of the dome on their elegant parallel boilers! However, once Mr Ivatt, or whoever added eighteen 2A conversions of the 52 original Patriots to the two Jubilees which had been rebuilt in 1943, and the Royal Scots that would eventually become rebuilds, took the bit between his teeth, there was engine picking to be had...

The Patriot rebuilds at first had what could be described as a rather angular top feed as per Stanier's design (or that of his officers). For reasons not yet unearthed (they probably never will be now) it was

6000, less than a year after its building, at Kentish Town in May 1934. It became 5538 and was named GIGGLESWICK towards the end of 1938.

5905 LORD RATHMORE at Kentish Town, in May 1934. Getting on for twenty of the Patriots went first of all to the Midland Division, at either Holbeck or Kentish Town, but very quickly they gravitated to the Western Division, which remained Patriot territory thereafter. Named from the first, LORD RATHMORE became 5533 under the 1934 arrangements.

decided to change the top feed cover from this 'angular' look to a more curved style which, it must be said, was a distinct improvement. This change seems to have followed on from Ivatt's taking of the reins, though presumably the layout inside the cover remained unaltered.

The changes appear, from photographic evidence, to have begun in the very late 1940s; indeed it seems fairly certain that some of the later rebuilds had the Ivatt version from the start. Completion seems to have come with 45532 in the middle of the golden decade the 1950s truly was. The

process now encompassed all of what had by then been re-classified as the 7P 4-6-0s. The changes from Stanier to Ivatt version seem to have been concurrent with the fitting of smoke deflectors to the rebuilds, but it would not take five minutes to unearth proof that there were exceptions to this very

5933 at its Home shed, Kentish Town (code 16). It was at Edge Hill (as 5521) by early 1935 and during its subsequent perambulations around the Western Division was named RHYL about 1937. Photograph The Transport Treasury.

6000 under construction at Crewe, more or less complete in a curiously deserted Erecting Shop. The piano front between the frames above the buffer beam is off, affording a view of the inside steamchest cover and valve spindle. What looks like the camera case lays on the ancient bench.

loose observation. If we were to take the various combinations of old LMS 1946 black, BR mixed traffic black, light green and Brunswick green and mix with every deflector fitment and top feed alteration, the eighteen rebuilds would give just about every combination possible!

**Bogies**
The first dozen Patriots, 5500-5511, had 6ft 3in bogies. This was of course the Claughton dimensions; presumably they were, in fact, ex-Claughton 'radial' bogies. The Jubilees built with short fireboxes at Crewe (5552-5556, 5607-5654) also took the

6ft 3in wheelbase bogies, following the Patriots. The rest of the Patriots got 6ft 6in Churchward/De Glehn bogies, as did the rest of the Jubilees.

**Clans?**
An important contribution to the canon of Patriot literature came in the first

One of the Patriots built new with the 5500 series numbers, though all the original details are there; curved deflectors from new, vacuum pump, drain pipes, no rain strip on cab. This is Kentish Town, with the engine in its first few weeks of life; by June 1934 5544 – never named – had moved on to Holbeck.

5547, another of the last ten Patriots to take the 5500 series from the first, in red livery. It entered traffic in April 1934 and was at Newton Heath by August. So, with its 26A plate this picture is after that time; there's been time enough to shorten the cylinder cock drain pipes but the vacuum pump is still in place. Would you call that tender unbeaded? Photograph W. Hermiston, The Transport Treasury.

*British Railways Illustrated Annual* way back in 1992... By February 1949 the total of eighteen taper boiler Patriot conversions was complete and it was a serious prediction that the coming BR mixed traffic light Pacific (later to manifest itself as the Clan) to be introduced in 1951, would make suitable replacements for the remaining thirty-four original Patriots. By now, against the taper boiler conversions, the Baby Scots certainly looked increasingly obsolescent, and a lot of heavy boiler renewal would soon become due. So it was that, as early as July 1949, a memorandum to the then Railway Executive proposed that any as-yet unconverted Patriot and Royal

A Patriot in Scotland; 45514 HOLYHEAD at Dalry Road shed, Edinburgh on 3 February 1951. It was a Camden engine by then so is very far from home indeed. Photograph J. Robertson, The Transport Treasury.

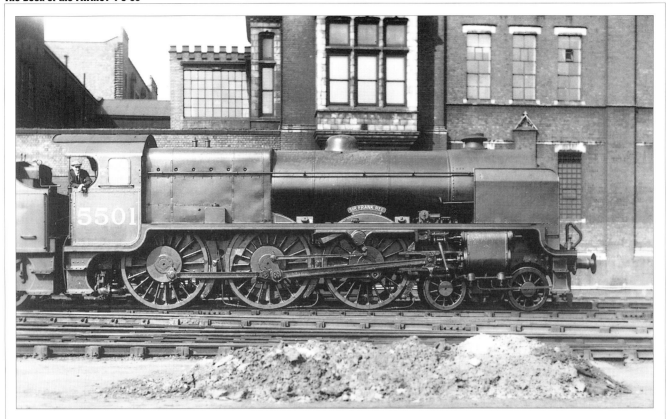

Scot 4-6-0s should not be rebuilt but replaced by the projected Pacific. This memorandum would mark the death-knell of the Grand Project of a vast 6P fleet of all the Scots, Patriots and Jubilees, converted with taper boilers. A rather curious further proposal, however, surfaced in April 1950; this seemed to envisage a sort of 'low calory' 2A Taper Boiler version of the Patriots, converting the remaining parallel boiler examples but with pressures at 200lb, so that they would still be power class 5X. We can only take this at face value… Obviously it was never followed through but it is a fascinating thought. It is reproduced opposite.

*Above and below.* Two sides of the early Patriot coin at Kentish Town in May 1934 – different sites for the '5XP', big wheel bosses on 5501, one of the two 'originals', both in red, fluted versus flat coupling rods. 5501 has coil springs on the leading drivers, 5963 has leaf springs. 5501 SIR FRANK REE had gone first to Crewe North and then Longsight and, unusually, had then moved to the Midland Division, going to Kentish Town in June 1932 (it was back on the Western Division before the end of 1935). It was renumbered into the 5500 series in April 1934, a few weeks before this picture; 5963 on the other hand, has yet to be renumbered, in a couple of months' time, in July 1934. It was a Holbeck engine and had come to the Midland Division new, though it was soon on its way along with the other Midland Division Patriots, going to Bushbury early in 1935.

**4-6-0 Class 5X 3-Cylinder Locomotives Nos.5500-5551**

*The 3-cylinder engines (between Nos.5500-5551) which still retain the original parallel boilers are dimensionally suitable for reboilering with standard 2A sloping throatplate taper boiler.*

*The following new details and alterations to the existing engines with parallel boiler will be necessary to make the conversion:-*

1. BOILER. *The standard 2A sloping throatplate taper boiler, with working pressure reduced from 250 to 200lb per sq. inch. The latter pressure enables the engine to retain its existing 5X classification. This boiler includes a rocking grate. Modifications required to foundation ring to suit new carrying arrangements.*

2. ASHPAN. *New ashpan. To be same as that fitted to Class 6 engines with 2A taper boiler. This ashpan has hopper doors incorporated. Damper gear to be redesigned to suit.*

3. CLOTHING. *New clothing. To be same as that fitted to 2A taper boiler.*

4. SMOKEBOX. *etc. New circular type smokebox in place of existing flat bottom type. Diameter (5ft 8½in inside) to be same as for Class 6 engines with 2A taper boiler, but length increased to suit.*

*New fabricated smokebox saddle fastened to inside cylinder at front end and resting on existing inside valve spindle guide stretcher casting at back end. New saddle to incorporate existing packing glands round blast pipe connections and inside steam pipe connection, etc. Existing blastpipe to be used again.*

*New steam pipes for inside and outside cylinders to suit header on 2A boiler. New steam pipe air tight joints on smokebox. New steam pipe connection pieces to cylinders to suit three bolt steam pipe flanges, and to accommodate new saddle.*

*The following new smokebox details which are required will be the same design as for existing Class 6 taper boiler engines:-*

> *Smokebox front end door complete.*
> *Steam pipe flanges and lens joints.*
> *Header supporting brackets.*

*A new design of single chimney and petticoat will be required as the ejector exhaust ring is incorporated in the existing blast pipe cap which is single. Alternatively a new double blast pipe could be fitted and the Class 6 double chimney retained.*

5. CAB. *The cut-away in cab front for the 2A firebox is smaller than that necessary for the existing parallel firebox, except on the top. A new cab front plate is therefore required with the profile of the front opening to suit the 2A boiler clothing. Making up pieces will be required for the reversing screw casing on L.H. side.*

*Wood platform arrangement (cab floor) to be modified to suit new firebox.*

6. MAINFRAMES. *Alterations are required to the main frames to suit carrying brackets at front of firebox. A modification is necessary to the front of hind dragbox to accommodate the firebox expansion plate, and to clear the injector steam and vacuum train pipes. This entails moving the vertical front plate back several inches and shortening the horizontal plates to suit.*

7. PIPES. *etc. Injector delivery pipes lengthened to connect up to top feed on taper boiler, injector steam pipes lengthened to suit manifold. New ejector required (same as for taper boiler engines).*

*Slight modifications will be necessary to the following items:-*

> *Splashers (angles to clothing altered).*
> *Sand box shield plates.*

GENERAL. *In assessing the above alterations required, it has been assumed that the minimum amount of alteration will be made to make the conversion.*

*Additional work to bring the Engine up to date would include the fitting of self cleaning smokebox plates and details which would be of new design to suit the internal arrangement of the smokebox.*

*The weights (in working order) will be approximately as follows:-*

*On leading bogie – 20 ton 10 cwt.*
*On leading coupled wheels – 20 ton 15 cwt.*
*On intermediate coupled wheels – 20 ton 15 cwt.*
*On trailing coupled wheels – 20 ton 0 cwt.*

**5520 LLANDUDNO in official garb. It had been named 'by January 1938' and this official view would have been taken to mark this event – by now the vacuum pump has gone (though the bracket remains) and the '5XP' is on the cab side, with cylinder drain pipes cut back. It carries an 8A Edge Hill shed plate; it had gone there in 1935. The tender is of the so-called 'unbeaded' variety though to identify unbeaded and beaded is not as easy as you'd think. Photograph Collection Ken Coventry.**

45541 DUKE OF SUTHERLAND, in the 'transitional' garb which characterised the period 1948-49. Underneath all that grime is post-war black lined straw and maroon, with serif smokebox number plate and BRITISH RAILWAYS on the tender. Photograph J. Robertson, The Transport Treasury.

BR mixed traffic lined black on 45549 (never named); pictured at Crewe North immediately after painting from the way the sun bounces off the cylinder casing and other parts. The sun also picks out the 'webs' on the short spokes leading off the crankpin; still '5XP', but positioned under the number. The webs were essentially a 'stiffening-up' device, a Great Western practice which presumably Stanier brought with him. The Royal Scots, Patriots and Jubilees all had 6ft 9in driving wheels with a 13 inch crank-throw so, to get an engine back into traffic as quickly as possible, Crewe was in the habit of fitting the next wheel-set to come to hand.

Begrimed BR black on **45516 THE BEDFORDSHIRE AND HERTFORDSHIRE REGIMENT**, at Upperby in August 1953. Photograph A.G. Ellis, The Transport Treasury.

## Tenders

The Patriots before rebuilding had 3,500 gallon tenders though (apart from the obvious high-sided ones – shown in the table, Nos.4569, 4570 and 4573) it is hard to tell which particular variety is which. The three types of standard Fowler tender – differentiating 1 and 2 often requires the luck of the light and the eye of faith – were:

1. Riveted and built with the locos, with beaded tanks.
2. Riveted and built with the locos, with non-beaded tanks.

Eighteen Patriots were 'rebuilt' with the new 2A taper boiler into a form hardly distinguishable from the converted Royal Scots and Jubilees. The cabs were different (the rebuilt Scots retained the Fowler cab; the rebuilt Patriots had a Stanier one) and there were steps *inside the frames* on the front of a Royal Scot but not on a Patriot; apart from numbers and plates these were the main 'long distance' methods of identification. Also, the buffer beam was deeper in the Patriots, rebuilt or not, than in the Scot. 5530 was the first Patriot converted, followed by 5521. As 45530 SIR FRANK REE (which had been 5501's name until 1937) it became perhaps the most celebrated Patriot at the end, being a prized inhabitant at Willesden. It was kept so well that correspondents to the railway press in 1963 assumed it was fresh from Crewe Works, Here it is at Willesden showing those powerful lines, 27 July 1963. Photograph Peter Groom.

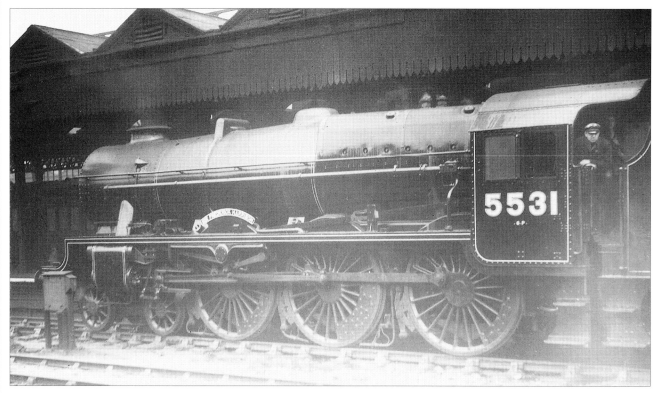

5531 SIR FREDERICK HARRISON in that gorgeous LMS black, at Crewe, as yet without the Royal Scot style smoke deflectors. 5524 had had this name from 1933 to 1937 when it passed to 5531. Photograph J.L. Stevenson, courtesy Hamish Stevenson.

3. Flush riveted type with beaded tanks originally attached to the Royal Scots and then transferred to the Jubilees. All except two of these were fitted with additional coal rails while running with a Baby Scot. The two exceptions were Nos.3187 and 3190. All three were designated 'Old Standard' from 1932.

Bizarrely, 5971 (5500) left Derby with its former ROD tender No.6309, which it had had as a Claughton and ran so fitted for about six weeks. *Brassmasters* with customary diligence,

5521 RHYL with town crest, in the famous black. This is Camden shed on 12 May 1948, the north end, with 5521's tender coaled up and the loco ready to back down to Euston. While with RHYL there is a good opportunity to examine the differences in top feed covers – compare with 45530 at Willesden for instance. Photograph Paul Chancellor Collection.

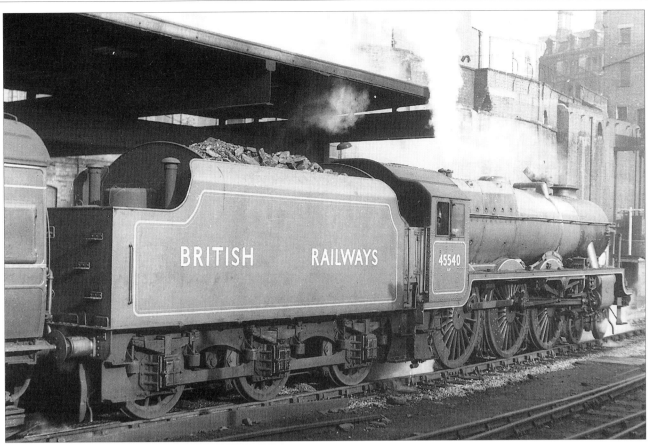

45540 SIR ROBERT TURNBULL at Birmingham New Street with the somewhat effete apple green livery; shortly afterwards, thankfully, it was quietly done away with. Photograph J.L. Stevenson, courtesy Hamish Stevenson.

Bushbury's 45525 COLWYN BAY (with town crest) in the fine BR black ('LNW black', or 'blackberry black') rushes past the Bourne End signals with the up 9.40am express from Wolverhampton. E.D. Bruton was notable for the immense detail and commentary he appended to his lovely board-backed prints. The speed was something like 60mph and the date 25 March 1950 at 12.15pm. Most of the visible part of the train was carmine and cream. The extra tall 'dolls' were so arranged that they could be seen at a distance over the little bridge. Photograph E.D. Bruton.

Table of tenders – original engines only

| Loco | Tend. | Type | Coal rails | Running from | Running to |
|---|---|---|---|---|---|
| 5500 | 3187 | Flush riveted | | 24/12/30 | 22/02/35 |
| 5516 | 3187 | Flush riveted | | 23/02/35 | 06/02/52 |
| 5541 | 3187 | Flush riveted | | 08/11/58 | 20/02/59 |
| 5501 | 3190 | Flush riveted | | 26/12/31 | 15/05/52 |
| 6502 | 3190 | Flush riveted | | 23/06/52 | 12/03/54 |
| 5505 | 3190 | Flush riveted | | 09/03/54 | 04/11/54 |
| 5513 | 3190 | Flush riveted | | 05/11/54 | 03/06/57 |
| 5545 | 3331 | Flush riveted | 16/04/37 | 06/04/48 | 04/11/48 |
| 5515 | 3898 | Flush riveted | Coal rails | 09/02/57 | 16/08/57 |
| 5544 | 3898 | Flush riveted | Coal rails | 17/08/57 | 04/12/57 |
| 5539 | 3899 | Flush riveted | 03/07/31 | 04/12/54 | 30/04/56 |
| 5537 | 3899 | Flush riveted | | 03/07/31 | 04/03/60 |
| 5502 | 3904 | Flush riveted | Coal rails | 14/09/56 | 13/09/57 |
| 5513 | 3907 | Flush riveted | Coal rails | 04/06/57 | 04/02/59 |
| 5544 | 3909 | Flush riveted | Coal rails | 18/05/32 | 02/07/56 16/08/57 |
| 5502 | 3909 | Flush riveted | Coal rails | 18/05/32 | 14/09/57 |
| 5538 | 3909 | Flush riveted | Coal rails | 18/05/32 | 07/10/60 |
| 5518 | 3913 | Flush riveted | Coal rails | 13/10/59 | |
| 5539 | 3922 | Flush riveted | Coal rails | 05/08/53 | 03/12/54 |
| 5508 | 3922 | Flush riveted | Coal rails | 13/01/55 | 06/12/56 |
| 5518 | 3922 | Flush riveted | Coal rails | 24/10/58 | 12/10/59 |
| 5513 | 3927 | Flush riveted | Coal rails | 09/09/32 | 05/10/50 02/12/53 |
| 5547 | 3927 | Flush riveted | Coal rails | 07/12/53 | 27/04/55 |
| 5542 | 3927 | Flush riveted | Coal rails | 09/09/32 | 09/06/55 18/11/60 |
| 5515 | 3927 | Flush riveted | Coal rails | 09/09/32 | 19/11/60 |
| 5516 | 3929 | Flush riveted | Coal rails | 07/02/52 | 28/12/53 |
| 5529 | 3931 | Flush riveted | Coal rails | 05/10/45 | 01/05/46 |
| 5511 | 3931 | Flush riveted | Coal rails | 10/10/53 | 02/03/55 |
| 5544 | 3931 | Flush riveted | Coal rails | 05/12/57 | 31/05/59 |
| 5550 | 3931 | Flush riveted | Coal rails | 01/06/59 | |
| 5500 | 3933 | Flush riveted | Coal rails | 17/03/55 | 15/06/56 |
| 5516 | 3933 | Flush riveted | Coal rails | 10/12/57 | 21/02/58 |
| 5511 | 3933 | Flush riveted | Coal rails | 22/02/58 | 01/09/60 |
| 5539 | 3937 | Flush riveted | Coal rails | 18/02/52 | 04/08/53 |
| 5511 | 3937 | Flush riveted | Coal rails | 03/03/55 | 21/02/58 |
| 5537 | 3943 | Flush riveted | Coal rails | 29/03/58 | 03/03/60 |
| 5547 | 3943 | Flush riveted | Coal rails | 27/02/60 | |
| 5501 | 4190 | Flush riveted | ? | 13/11/30 | 25/12/31 |
| 5513 | 4236 | Flush riveted | Coal rails | 03/12/53 | 04/11/54 |
| 5505 | 4236 | Flush riveted | Coal rails | 05/11/54 | 01/04/60 |
| 5547 | 4238 | Flush riveted | Coal rails | 17/01/59 | 26/02/60 |
| 5550 | 4242 | Flush riveted | Coal rails | 23/01/56 | 30/07/56 |
| 5551 | 4242 | Flush riveted | Coal rails | 31/07/56 | 01/05/58 |
| 5541 | 4248 | Flush riveted | Coal rails | 17/04/50 | 03/12/52 |
| 5507 | 4248 | Flush riveted | Coal rails | 15/05/59 | |
| 5511 | 4252 | Flush riveted | Coal rails | 02/09/60 | |
| 5542 | 4469 | Riveted unbeaded | Coal rails | 13/03/34 | 12/12/38 |
| 5536 | 4469 | Riveted unbeaded | Coal rails | 03/12/38 | 10/01/39 |
| 5542 | 4469 | Riveted unbeaded | Coal rails | 11/01/39 | 29/01/44 |
| 5542 | 4469 | Riveted unbeaded | Coal rails | 22/03/44 | 08/06/55 |
| 5541 | 4469 | Riveted unbeaded | Coal rails | 18/08/55 | 07/11/58 |
| 5543 | 4470 | Riveted unbeaded | Coal rails | 16/03/34 | 14/12/35 |
| 5544 | 4470 | Riveted unbeaded | Coal rails | 15/12/35 | 05/03/50 |
| 5544 | 4471 | Riveted unbeaded | Coal rails | 22/03/34 | 14/12/35 |
| 5543 | 4471 | Riveted unbeaded | Coal rails | 15/12/35 | 27/06/56 |
| 5545 | 4472 | Riveted unbeaded | Coal rails | 27/03/34 | 05/04/48 |
| 5546 | 4473 | Riveted unbeaded | Coal rails | 29/03/34 | 14/10/54 |
| 5507 | 4473 | Riveted unbeaded | Coal rails | 15/10/54 | 14/05/59 |
| 5502 | 4474 | Riveted beaded | Coal rails | 01/07/32 | 22/06/52 |
| 5520 | 4474 | Riveted beaded | Coal rails | 14/10/52 | 06/03/55 |
| 5503 | 4475 | Riveted beaded | Coal rails | 01/07/32 | 20/07/34 |
| 5512 | 4475 | Riveted beaded | Coal rails | 21/07/34 | 20/09/34 |
| 5503 | 4475 | Riveted beaded | Coal rails | 21/09/34 | 02/05/58 |
| 5550 | 4475 | Riveted beaded | Coal rails | 03/05/58 | 31/05/59 |
| 5544 | 4475 | Riveted beaded | Coal rails | 01/06/59 | |
| 5504 | 4476 | Riveted beaded | Coal rails | 18/07/53 | |
| 5505 | 4477 | Riveted beaded | Coal rails | 26/07/32 | 08/03/54 |
| 5541 | 4477 | Riveted beaded | Coal rails | 28/04/54 | 17/08/55 |
| 5506 | 4478 | Riveted beaded | Coal rails | 01/08/32 | |
| 5508 | 4479 | Riveted beaded | Coal rails | 09/08/32 | 12/01/55 |
| 5520 | 4479 | Riveted beaded | Coal rails | 07/03/55 | 22/01/56 |
| 5543 | 4479 | Riveted beaded | Coal rails | 28/06/56 | |
| 5507 | 4480 | Riveted beaded | Coal rails | 12/08/32 | 14/10/54 |
| 5546 | 4480 | Riveted beaded | Coal rails | 15/10/54 | |
| 5509 | 4481 | Riveted beaded | Coal rails | 19/08/32 | |
| 5510 | 4482 | Riveted beaded | Coal rails | 24/08/32 | 12/05/61 |
| 5520 | 4482 | Riveted beaded | Coal rails | 13/05/61 | |
| 5511 | 4483 | Riveted beaded | Coal rails | 31/08/32 | 09/10/53 |
| 5500 | 4483 | Riveted beaded | Coal rails | 05/02/54 | 16/03/55 |
| 5512 | 4484 | Riveted beaded | Coal rails | 14/09/32 | 06/07/34 |
| 5528 | 4484 | Riveted beaded | Coal rails | 07/07/34 | 20/07/34 |
| 5503 | 4484 | Riveted beaded | Coal rails | 21/07/34 | 20/09/34 |
| 5512 | 4484 | Riveted beaded | Coal rails | 21/09/34 | 25/07/48 |
| 5513 | 4485 | Riveted beaded | Coal rails | 19/09/32 | 04/11/41 |
| 5521 | 4485 | Riveted beaded | Coal rails | 22/10/44 | 30/10/46 |
| 5514 | 4486 | Riveted beaded | Coal rails | 21/09/32 | 14/03/47 |
| 5515 | 4487 | Riveted beaded | Coal rails | 27/09/32 | 28/07/53 |
| 5537 | 4487 | Riveted beaded | Coal rails | 29/06/54 | 28/03/58 |
| 5515 | 4487 | Riveted beaded | Coal rails | 15/03/58 | 02/04/59 |
| 5503 | 4487 | Riveted beaded | Coal rails | 23/04/59 | |
| 5516 | 4488 | Riveted beaded | Coal rails | 10/10/32 | 22/02/35 |
| 5500 | 4488 | Riveted beaded | Coal rails | 23/02/35 | 04/02/54 |
| 5502 | 4488 | Riveted beaded | Coal rails | 13/03/54 | 13/09/56 |
| 5508 | 4488 | Riveted beaded | Coal rails | 07/12/56 | |
| 5533 | 4488 | Riveted beaded | Coal rails | 15/03/61 | |
| 5517 | 4489 | Riveted unbeaded | Coal rails | 06/02/33 | 24/10/60 |
| 5515 | 4489 | Riveted unbeaded | Coal rails | 25/10/60 | 18/11/60 |
| 5542 | 4489 | Riveted unbeaded | Coal rails | 19/11/60 | |
| 5518 | 4490 | Riveted unbeaded | Coal rails | 20/02/33 | 23/10/58 |
| 5513 | 4490 | Riveted unbeaded | Coal rails | 05/02/59 | |
| 5519 | 4491 | Riveted unbeaded | Coal rails | 25/02/33 | |
| 5523 | 4492 | Riveted unbeaded | Coal rails | 08/03/33 | 07/03/45 |
| 5522 | 4492 | Riveted unbeaded | Coal rails | 08/03/45 | 30/12/48 |
| 5547 | 4492 | Riveted unbeaded | Coal rails | 28/04/55 | 16/01/59 |
| 5524 | 4493 | Riveted unbeaded | Coal rails | 14/03/33 | 16/08/54 |
| 5503 | 4493 | Riveted unbeaded | Coal rails | 03/05/58 | 22/04/59 |
| 5515 | 4493 | Riveted unbeaded | Coal rails | 05/05/59 | 24/10/60 |
| 5517 | 4493 | Riveted unbeaded | Coal rails | 25/10/60 | |
| 5530 | 4494 | Riveted unbeaded | Coal rails | 03/04/33 | 18/10/46 |
| 5529 | 4495 | Riveted unbeaded | Coal rails | 06/04/33 | 04/10/45 |
| 5529 | 4495 | Riveted unbeaded | Coal rails | 02/05/46 | 04/07/47 |
| 5531 | 4496 | Riveted unbeaded | Coal rails | 07/04/33 | 12/12/47 |
| 5532 | 4497 | Riveted unbeaded | Coal rails | 11/04/33 | 02/07/48 |
| 5544 | 4497 | Riveted unbeaded | Coal rails | 03/04/54 | 01/07/56 |
| 5536 | 4498 | Riveted unbeaded | Coal rails | 04/05/33 | 12/12/38 |
| 5542 | 4498 | Riveted unbeaded | Coal rails | 13/12/38 | 10/01/39 |
| 5536 | 4498 | Riveted unbeaded | Coal rails | 11/01/39 | 11/11/48 |
| 5520 | 4499 | Riveted unbeaded | Coal rails | 17/02/33 | 13/10/52 |
| 5541 | 4499 | Riveted unbeaded | Coal rails | 04/12/52 | 27/04/54 |
| 5521 | 4500 | Riveted beaded | Coal rails | 24/02/33 | 21/10/44 |
| 5513 | 4500 | Riveted beaded | Coal rails | 05/11/41 | 04/10/50 |
| 5541 | 4500 | Riveted beaded | Coal rails | 21/02/59 | |
| 5522 | 4501 | Riveted beaded | Coal rails | 03/03/33 | 07/03/45 |
| 5523 | 4501 | Riveted beaded | Coal rails | 08/03/45 | 07/11/48 |
| 5526 | 4502 | Riveted beaded | Coal rails | 22/03/33 | 27/12/46 |
| 5525 | 4503 | Riveted beaded | Coal rails | 22/03/33 | 19/08/48 |
| 5527 | 4504 | Riveted beaded | Coal rails | 27/03/33 | 12/09/48 |
| 5528 | 4505 | Riveted beaded | Coal rails | 04/04/33 | 06/07/34 |
| 5512 | 4505 | Riveted beaded | Coal rails | 07/07/34 | 20/07/34 |
| 5528 | 4505 | Riveted beaded | Coal rails | 21/07/34 | 20/08/47 |
| 5542 | 4505 | Riveted beaded | Coal rails | 30/01/44 | 21/03/44 |
| 5515 | 4505 | Riveted beaded | Coal rails | 29/07/53 | 03/01/56 |
| 5520 | 4505 | Riveted beaded | Coal rails | 23/01/56 | 12/05/61 |
| 5510 | 4505 | Riveted beaded | Coal rails | 13/05/61 | |
| 5533 | 4506 | Riveted beaded | Coal rails | 10/04/33 | 14/03/61 |
| 5534 | 4507 | Riveted beaded | Coal rails | 25/04/33 | 30/12/48 |
| 5535 | 4508 | Riveted beaded | Coal rails | 04/05/33 | 24/09/48 |
| 5537 | 4509 | Riveted unbeaded | Coal rails | 19/07/33 | 28/06/54 |
| 5524 | 4509 | Riveted unbeaded | Coal rails | 17/08/54 | 25/11/55 |
| 5515 | 4509 | Riveted unbeaded | Coal rails | 04/01/56 | 09/01/57 |
| 5539 | 4509 | Riveted unbeaded | Coal rails | 10/01/57 | |
| 5538 | 4510 | Riveted unbeaded | Coal rails | 21/07/33 | 22/08/56 |
| 5550 | 4510 | Riveted unbeaded | Coal rails | 23/08/56 | 02/05/58 |
| 5539 | 4511 | Riveted unbeaded | Coal rails | 27/07/33 | 17/02/52 |
| 5501 | 4511 | Riveted unbeaded | Coal rails | 16/05/52 | |
| 5540 | 4512 | Riveted unbeaded | Coal rails | 07/08/33 | 31/10/47 |
| 5524 | 4512 | Riveted unbeaded | Coal rails | 26/11/55 | |
| 5541 | 4513 | Riveted unbeaded | Coal rails | 15/08/33 | 16/04/50 |
| 5547 | 4554 | Riveted unbeaded | Coal rails | 09/04/34 | 06/12/53 |
| 5516 | 4554 | Riveted unbeaded | Coal rails | 29/12/53 | 09/12/57 |
| 5516 | 4554 | Riveted unbeaded | Coal rails | 22/02/58 | |
| 5548 | 4555 | Riveted unbeaded | Coal rails | 27/04/34 | |
| 5549 | 4556 | Riveted unbeaded | Coal rails | 27/04/34 | |
| 5550 | 4557 | Riveted unbeaded | Coal rails | 01/05/34 | 28/12/42 |
| 5500 | 4557 | Riveted unbeaded | Coal rails | 16/06/56 | |
| 5551 | 4558 | Riveted unbeaded | Coal rails | 02/05/34 | 19/09/34 |
| 5551 | 4558 | Riveted unbeaded | Coal rails | 04/10/34 | 30/07/56 |
| 5550 | 4558 | Riveted unbeaded | Coal rails | 31/07/56 | 22/08/56 |
| 5538 | 4558 | Riveted unbeaded | Coal rails | 23/08/56 | 06/10/60 |
| 5551 | 4560 | Riveted unbeaded | Coal rails | 20/09/34 | 03/10/34 |
| 5544 | 4561 | Riveted unbeaded | Coal rails | 06/03/50 | 02/04/54 |
| 5505 | 4569 | High sided | | 02/04/60 | |
| 5515 | 4570 | High sided | | 17/08/57 | 14/03/58 |
| 5551 | 4570 | High sided | | 02/05/58 | |
| 5550 | 4573 | High sided | | 29/12/42 | 22/01/56 |
| 5539 | 4573 | High sided | | 01/05/56 | 09/01/57 |
| 5515 | 4573 | High sided | | 10/01/57 | 08/02/57 |
| 5500 | 6309 | Ex ROD | | 08/11/30 | 23/12/30 |

have tabulated much of all this, in connection with their wonderful Patriot etched brass kit and I am infinitely grateful, once again, to be able to reproduce the data.

Some sixteen locomotives, it turns out, had the same tender throughout from building to rebuilding or withdrawal. The proportion of each of the three types of standard tender was more or less 1:1:1 over the life of the class although the riveted varieties were more common in the first few years.

The eighteen engines converted with taper boilers all got welded 4,000 gallon tenders in the 9700 series. They carried nine tons of coal and could be interchanged with Royal Scots or Jubilees.

## Liveries

Patriot livery was probably every bit the spawn of the devil as the Jubilees, individuals in the class bearing every twist and turn of LMS livery from the 1930s. What follows is a general outline; once again, if an engine is to be tied to a particular year, a photograph is the only 100% sure way. What follows will be familiar to readers of *The Book of the Jubilee 4-6-0s*.

1. The first Patriots were red* with black and yellow lining. This meant

*Above and top.* 45523 BANGOR and 45535 SIR HERBERT WALKER K.C.B. at their home shed Crewe North in 1950 in a livery assumed to be BR lined black. The two Patriots had emerged as taper boiler conversions in October and September 1948 re-spectively. My guess is that Willie Hermiston took both these pictures on the same day in 1950; behind 45535 is the ancient LNW mech-anical coaling plant, dating back to 1909 while in the distance to the right of 45523 are the scaffolded beginnings of the BR replacement. Photographs
W. Hermiston, The Transport Treasury.

the 1928 insignia, 12 inch numerals on the cab and 14 inch L M S on the tenders. Minor differences arose between Crewe and Derby built/ painted engines, however. Those from Crewe had slightly closer lettering on the tender and the cab side 5XP was between the window and the rear cut-out. The cab side numbers were twelve inches high. Derby had the LMS on the tender at a rather wider spacing and the 5XP was in front of the window. This contrast disappeared when the wind deflector was added, the 5XP moving to a site below the window. Derby used 14 inch numbers on the cab side; the spacing was to take account of rivet runs and the 'Derby 14 inch' numbers seem to have died out with the 1934 renumbering

*Red: good enough for most of us though 'crimson lake' is insisted upon by some. The shade is said to have weathered poorly but this may have more to do with the fact that the LMS was more frugal than others with repaints. An engine was obliged to perform longer between them than its contemporaries elsewhere. This is what probably produced the faded effect.*

2. In 1936-1938 new and repainted engines begin to get plain lettering and numbering in place of the scroll type. These were made up of 10 inch gold with red shading numbers and 14 inch L M S on the tenders.

3. From 1938 some numbers and letters revert to scroll type.

4. War sees the 'utility' black applied from 1940. The 'wartime black' is unlined with yellow shading letters and numbers. Few engines, it would seem, got anything like a full repaint in the war years, so many survived with pre-war red. A few survived right to Nationalisation like this, just as a number of Jubilees did.

5. The famously elegant LMS 1946 (applied until late 1948, latterly with BR markings) lined black with maroon and straw lining and block 12 inch numbers with 14 inch L M S appears, though by no means all the Patriots are so treated. The cab side number is moved upwards. With BR a few of the original engines get LNWR-style (often, perhaps more accurately, called 'BR mixed traffic') lined black; the first nine or ten taper boiler engines get the 1946 livery, the rest, apparently, emerged in the LNW lined black. These latter examples carry BRITISH RAILWAYS on the tender.

From studying photographs and conversion dates, we can say that the first livery bestowed on these eighteen conversions was, in order of emergence: LMS 1946 style lined black: 5521, 5530, 5526, 5514, 5529, 5528, 5540, 5531, 45512, 45532. These appeared

ex-works between October 1946 and July 1948.

BR mixed traffic lined black: 45525, 45527, 45535, 45523, 45536, 45545, 45534, 45522 ex-works between August 1948 and January 1949.

45531 and 45540 bear the experimental apple green for a while from mid-1948.

6. 'M' appears in front of the number on many LM engines in the first months of nationalisation, with BRITISH RAILWAYS on the tender and of course the universal application of 40,000 to the numbers. Surprisingly, I have not come across a photograph of a Patriot of either denomination so altered, though it certainly happened to Jubilees, Royal Scots, and others. Certainly a list of 'M' numbers in the SLS *Journal* 1948/49 did not include any Patriots – though it is tempting fate to rule it out altogether...

7. From mid-1949, 'GWR' Brunswick green takes hold and this is probably the only livery which all fifty-two carried at the same time. They have the first emblem; the second version appears from 1957.

## 6P-7P

The original Patriots kept the 5XP classification, it would seem, until 1951. In that year they became 6P while the 6P taper boiler engines became 7P, along with the rebuilt Royal Scots and the two Jubilee rebuilds. From 1955 the originals were officially 6P5F but the engines continued to carry just 6P on the cab.

## AWS

Most of the Patriots, and certainly all the taper boiler examples, were fitted with BR standard Automatic Warning System (AWS) equipment in 1959/60. In terms of visible detail differences there was the usual vacuum reservoir cylinder on the right-hand running plate with a smaller timing reservoir on the left-hand side. There was also the protection plate for the receiver under the buffer beam and the conduit (carrying the wiring) clipped to the left-hand running plate. On the original engines the battery box for the system was placed immediately in front of the cab, on the right-hand side but there was not sufficient room on the rebuilt ones, with the big 2A boiler so, as on the Royal Scots and Jubilees, the battery box went out of sight in the cab, under the driver's seat. AWS care (essentially, battery change) took place at the 3-5 week exam. A Concentration Shed like Crewe North would have a small room or caged-off area with charging equipment and lots of spare sets of batteries. They were alkali cells, two wooden boxes of six each, coupled in series to give the nominal 12 volts. It would be one of the older fitters' jobs

to look after them and there were always plenty of spare sets, but they were changed as an 'exam' item. Occasionally they would be changed 'out of course', if the AWS was reported defective. The AWS was also tested by hand magnet as a part of the daily exam, on all engines working Class 1 or 2 trains.

Latter day forms among the taper boiler engines, as illustrated by 45528. Peculiarly, 45528 had only been named as late as October 1959, R.E.M.E. The two views show 45528 first of all at Camden (below) in April 1959 when it was a Crewe North engine, and secondly (top right) at Willesden, about 1961-62. By the time of its transfer to Willesden it has acquired the second type of emblem on the tender, electrification flashes and AWS. Photographs The Transport Treasury.

# The Record

As pointed out in all the volumes of this series, *The Books of* the BR Standards, Coronations, Royal Scots, Princess Royals, Merchant Navys and West Countrys/Battle of Britains, railway company Engine Record Cards, while containing much useful and even fascinating information, should be regarded as a *guide* to what happened to the engines, not an unimpeachable document to be afforded the status of gospel. It seems to be stating the obvious that the Record Cards only show what was written on them at the time but the temptation to read and interpret too much should be resisted. As pointed out before in books in this series, the Cards are a marvellous, fascinating, invaluable record of what happened but they are often infuriatingly silent on events that we enthusiasts half a century or more later deem of vital interest and importance. Of 45508's stovepipe chimney for instance there is only silence, yet there are endless references to things like firebox door light shields, costing a few shillings and pence. They were filled in, by hand, by humans and naturally enough contain errors of omission (quite a few) and commission (a few).

These days, when the touch of a computer key can bring up a loco's repair and maintenance history in a trice (yet even these details are only as good as the ones that were entered in the first place) it requires something of an effort to imagine the never ending paper chase of the steam railway which, over years must have produced, literally, whole mountain ranges of paper (even if they did, by habit, often re-use the reverse side of an earlier document). The various Works had records for each engine, the sheds had records, there were records for boilers and tenders and other, non-Motive Power, departments had records too. A four-weekly statement went out to all and sundry announcing the details of loco transfers; in the meantime each shed got its own notification, when and where an engine was to go and if and when a replacement would arrive. It is curious, and not generally known that, on the LM at least, a shed would be instructed to transfer an engine *of a particular type*, 'a 4F 0-6-0' or whatever. A shed was *not* instructed to transfer a *specified individual loco*. The Shed Foreman was to an extent honour-bound to send one in decent nick. It was 'custom and practice', in BR days at

least, to send the last engine that was ex-works – though there were many transgressions. It was a calculated risk; if the recipient felt aggrieved there was the certainty that he would get his revenge in time. Once the engine was sent, the Foreman would forward the actual engine number to Derby. It was from these 'returns' that the four-weekly 'reallocation' lists were made up. *The Railway Observer* for one was obviously unofficially on the circulation list, hence the immediacy and accuracy of its material.

It is the survival of bundles of this sort of stuff that has perhaps convinced people that a 'day by day' picture of affairs, at some subtle level of accuracy not possible in any other circumstance, is possible. Certain 'runs' still exist for certain sheds, of course, and these are always fascinating but there is no single comprehensive *and manageable* body of data to match the Record Cards which go back, in some instances, to the 1920s. The whole system worked very well but we can never 'know' (except in a tiny minority of instances when personal diary observations are concerned) the specifics, right down to the accuracy of a certain day or time.

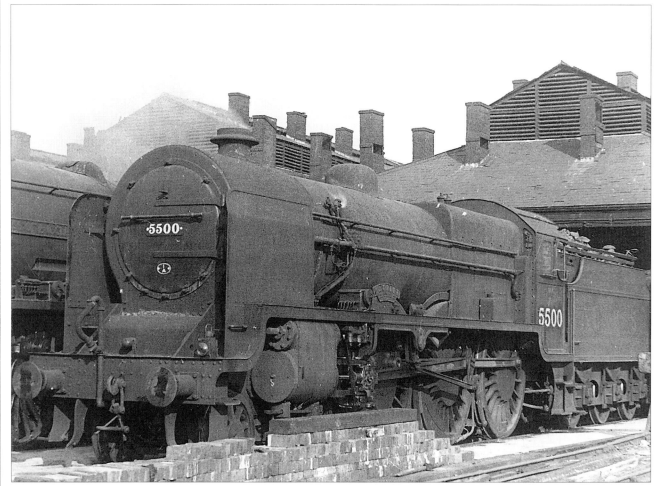

5500 PATRIOT at Willesden shed, 26 June 1946; equally scruffy DUCHESS OF BUCCLEUCH alongside. Photograph H.C. Casserley.

45500, with those ex-Claughton large wheel bosses, departs Manchester London Road with empty stock to Longsight sidings, 31 March 1954. Photograph B.K.B. Green, Initial Photographics.

A yet further type of record was the 'casualty sheet' which sought to explain and assign (or avoid!) blame for every failure or loss of time. 45505 THE ROYAL ARMY ORDNANCE CORPS for instance, was having a lot of trouble with its exhaust injector in the autumn of 1951. It had to come off its train at Carstairs on 31 October; the 'choked waterways' were cleared out and a 'new renewable cone end' fitted. Less than a week earlier, on 26 October it had failed at Preston with 'exhaust injector very unreliable'; repairs had been effected. The engine had only been transferred from Preston to Upperby a few weeks before; its new owners were obviously asked for an explanation and replied, seemingly stung, that 45505 had worked to Crewe on 26th and had not appeared again at Upperby (working from Glasgow!) until 1 November. There then follows fantastic detail as to 45505's daily and periodic exams, and it is a comfort to find all the dates and mileages agreeing with the Engine Record Card.

Dates of leaving and entry to Works were to an extent nominal and a day or two either side should always be assumed. Worse, the works were not above 'fiddling' dates slightly at the beginning or the end of a month to enhance the monthly figures, to match a quota either of 'engines in' or 'engines out'. It was thus far from entirely unknown for a locomotive to be still in works while shown 'out on the road' or even vice versa – for a few days at least.

Breathless 'shocks' and 'revelations' in the railway press about the occasional contradictions, Record Card *versus* sightings are great fun, but only that.

## Sheds

The sheds would keep mileages as part of a clerk's duties but once the monthly returns went to HQ they were either neglected or ignored. The record had to be kept to comply with Board of Trade safety regulations – moving parts had to be examined on a mileage basis. Mileages were to a great extent nominal – for example engines on ballast workings were allocated a set mileage irrespective of the distance they actually ran. This continued with diesels right to the end of BR – one TOPS hour per diagram! The point is, while a figure of 100,000 miles, say, might be argued over – was it 'really' 95,000 or 105,000? – mileages generally were comparable from engine to engine in a given class. As with all BR steam locomotives, the record fades from about 1959-60 as the people involved realised their charges were on the way out. Mileage recording in any event tended to fall apart once it was clear steam was doomed and no one bothered to record the last 'seeing out' mileages. The fundamentalists can argue about this but, curiously, even these final figures too, in the end, show a 'true' picture – mileage did decline (often precipitously) as locos sat around unfixed or whiled away the time on pick-up goods. The same was true of

allocations and many shed transfers at the end, while they were mostly recorded in the pages of contemporary magazines and journals, did not find their way onto the Record Cards. These 'last gasp' allocations (sometimes meaningless paper ones) have nevertheless been added at the end of the 'Sheds' section in the individual Tables.

## Works

It is a surprising thing but the LMS Record Cards do not specifically denote the particular works carrying out the repairs. A tiny minority of individual repairs/overhauls *do* have a particular works attached to the period of the job itself and these are duly noted. With some classes it is simple; all the Pacifics, for instance, whether Western or Northern Division, LMR or ScR, were overhauled (apart from some exceptional repairs) at Crewe. The same was true of the Royal Scots but larger, more widely dispersed classes, were different. The English Jubilees were certainly overhauled at Crewe, with Derby doing some of the more Casual work while Scottish ones were done at St Rollox. The Patriots, concentrated within a few years on the Western Division, would have been in the care of Crewe throughout their lives.

## Works Codes

Classification of works jobs varied over the years and the best we have come up with is: **HG** Heavy General; **NC** Non-Classified; **LS** Light Service and **HS** Heavy Service. These last two evolved by BR times into **LI** Light Intermediate and **HI** Heavy Intermediate. Terms changed or were misapplied by staff coming from other traditions; **LO** would thus be Light Overhaul and **LC** Light Casual. One extra since the days of *The Book of the Coronation Pacifics* is the **Rect** which simply means 'rectification' and typically took place a day or two after a major repair – that is, tightening up bits that had come loose and loosening bits that were too tight. They seldom took very long – often only a day. **(EO)** was 'Engine Order', under which some jobs seem to have been ordered out of the normal run of things.

The Record Cards represent an unmatched body of endlessly fascinating data, and if the reader gets half as much fun perusing the information as I have had in compiling it, I'll be content.

*Right.* **The ST DUNSTAN'S plate, an unusual badge device. Note again the large ex-Claughton wheel bosses.**

# 45500 PATRIOT

**Rebuilt Derby 8/11/30 from 5971 CROXTETH (LNWR CLAUGHTON No 2511 CROXTETH) Renamed PATRIOT 25/2/1937**
*Renumbered 5971 to 5500 3/5/34*
*5500 to 45500 week ending 23/4/49*

## MILEAGES

| | |
|---|---|
| 1930 | 1,589 |
| 1931 | 59,252 |
| 1932 | 69,827 |
| 1933 | 50,818 |
| 1934 | 59,315 |
| 1935 | 61,660 |
| 1936 | 65,459 |
| 1937 | 67,860 |
| 1938 | 62,606 |
| 1939 | 51,518 |
| 1940 | 37,478 |
| 1941 | 37,595 |
| 1942 | 41,023 |
| 1943 | 34,150 |
| 1944 | 38,913 |
| 1945 | 29,517 |
| 1946 | 21,156 |
| 1947 | 28,498 |
| 1948 | 37,061 |
| 1949 | 28,689 |
| 1950 | 22,586 |
| 1951 | 31,559 |
| 1952 | 39,321 |
| 1953 | 32,433 |
| 1954 | 40,043 |
| 1955 | 33,002 |
| 1956 | 34,109 |
| 1957 | 28,783 |
| 1958 | 29,847 |
| 1959 | 34,035 |
| 1960 | 26,591 |
| 1961 | 3,611 |

**Mileage at 31/12/50 906,570 Lifetime**
**Mileage 1,239,904**
**Withdrawn week ending 11/3/61**
**from Newton Heath**
**Scrap Details Broken Up 30/3/61**
**Scrapped Crewe Works 4/61**

## SHEDS

Leeds 8/11/30
Kentish Town 21/5/32
Camden 16/2/35
Crewe North 20/2/37
Camden 10/4/37
Willesden 20/11/37
Edge Hill 3/5/47
Longsight 5/6/48
Carlisle Upperby 6/11/54
Blackpool 26/7/58
Willesden 4/10/58
Carnforth 3/10/59
Newton Heath (Loan) 26/3/60
Newton Heath 28/5/60

## BOILERS

| Fitted | Number | Received From | When Removed Passed To |
|---|---|---|---|
| 8/11/30 | | | STOCK |
| 18/1/33 | | 5957 | STOCK |
| 19/4/34 | | 5927 | 5908 |
| 14/1/36 | | 5508 | 5522 |
| 29/11/37 | 6012 | 5537 | 5539 |
| 24/2/40 | 5985 | 5529 | 5520 |
| 21/12/43 | 5993 | 5542 | 5546 |
| 18/1/47 | 5988 | 5521 | 45543 |
| 8/3/52 | 5483 | 45527 | 45502 |
| 3/6/57 | 6012 | 45541 | WDL |

## TENDERS

| No | Fitted |
|---|---|
| 6309 | 8/11/30 (ex ROD) |
| 3187 | 24/12/30 |
| 4488 | 23/2/35 |
| 4483 | 5/2/54 |
| 3933 | 17/3/55 |
| 4557 | 16/6/56 |

## REPAIRS

17/12/30-24/12/30**LO** (7)
1/10/31-22/10/31**LS** (19)
14/4/32-10/5/32**LO** (23)
7/1/33-22/2/33**HG** (40)
25/10/33-24/11/33**LS** (27)
7/3/34-3/5/34**HS** (49)
11/2/35-5/3/35**HS** (20)
3/1/36-30/1/36**HG** (24)
12/2/37-25/2/37**HS** (12)
31/10/37-15/12/37**HG** (40)
21/7/38-22/8/38**LO** (28)
1/12/38-11/1/39**LS** (36)
5/8/39-15/8/39**LO** (9)
5/2/40-24/2/40**HG** (18)
4/6/40-18/6/40**LO** (13)
13/3/42-28/3/42**LS** (14)
3/12/43-21/12/43**HG** (16)
29/11/44-12/12/44**LS** (12)
7/9/45-6/10/45**LO** (26)
16/8/46-21/9/46**LS** (32)
9/12/46-18/1/47**HO** (35)
4/6/47-5/7/47**LO** (28)
13/10/47-22/11/47**LS** (36)
21/3/49-19/4/49**HI** (25)
25/4/49-20/5/49**NC(Rect)** (23)
28/9/49-22/10/49**LC** (22)
20/11/50-20/12/50**HI** (26)
12/1/52-8/3/52**HG** (48)
16/1/54-5/2/54**LI** (17)
28/1/55-17/3/55**HI** (41)
28/3/55-22/4/55**NC(Rect)EO** (21)
23/4/56-16/6/56**HC** (47)
19/7/56-25/7/56**NC(EO)** (5)
19/4/57-3/6/57**HG** (37)
12/6/57-21/6/57**NC(Rect)EO** (8)
4/11/57-11/12/57**LC(EO)** (32)
4/1/58-10/2/58**LC(EO)** (31)
11/11/58-13/12/58**LI** (28)
4/8/59-16/9/59**LC(EO)** (37) AWS
GEAR FITTED

# 45501 ST DUNSTAN'S

Rebuilt Derby 13/11/30 from 5902 SIR FRANK REE (LNWR
CLAUGHTON No.1191 SIR FRANK REE)
Renamed ST DUNSTAN'S 17/4/37
*Renumbered 5902 to 5501 12/4/34*
*5501 to 45501 week ending 26/3/49*

### BOILERS

| Fitted | Number | Received From | When Removed Passed To |
|--------|--------|--------------|------------------------|
| 13/11/30 | | | 5953 |
| 21/4/32 | | 5948 | STOCK |
| 14/3/34 | | 6005 | STOCK |
| 31/1/36 | 5998 | 5986 | 5536 |
| 20/9/37 | 6011 | 5529 | 5535 |
| 16/2/40 | 6174 | 5516 | 5529 |
| 7/11/42 | 5480 | 5530 | |
| 13/9/47 | 5357 | 5514 | 45501 |
| 16/5/52 | 5357 | 45501 | 45509 |
| 2/2/54 | 5978 | 45547 | 45524 |
| 15/12/56 | 6176 | 45550 | WDL |

### SHEDS

Crewe North 13/11/30
Longsight 28/10/31
Kentish Town 18/6/32
Leeds 30/10/33
Camden 11/35
Crewe North 20/2/37
Camden 10/4/37
Crewe North 26/11/38
Camden (Loan) 10/12/38
Camden 31/12/38
Willesden 10/6/39
Crewe North 22/3/41
Longsight (Loan) 14/3/42
Crewe North 28/3/42
Preston 11/4/42
Patricroft 6/6/42
Edge Hill 3/10/42
Willesden 16/6/45
Edge Hill 3/5/47
Longsight 5/6/48
Crewe North 14/6/58
Carnforth 7/11/59
Mold Jct 23/1/60
Warrington 23/4/60
Carlisle Upperby 10/9/60

### MILEAGES

| Year | Mileage |
|------|---------|
| 1930 | 3,767 |
| 1931 | 46,754 |
| 1932 | 56,601 |
| 1933 | 54,687 |
| 1934 | 64,964 |
| 1935 | 56,668 |
| 1936 | 67,161 |
| 1937 | 61,762 |
| 1938 | 58,945 |
| 1939 | 63,032 |
| 1940 | 38,756 |
| 1941 | 38,250 |
| 1942 | 37,054 |
| 1943 | 43,352 |
| 1944 | 33,419 |
| 1945 | 23,605 |
| 1946 | 27,180 |
| 1947 | 27,389 |
| 1948 | 33,742 |
| 1949 | 35,722 |
| 1950 | 17,682 |
| 1951 | 36,591 |
| 1952 | 27,892 |
| 1953 | 37,603 |
| 1954 | 35,954 |
| 1955 | 33,171 |
| 1956 | 39,742 |
| 1957 | 50,259 |
| 1958 | 33,281 |
| 1959 | 28,850 |
| 1960 | 34,367 |
| 1961 | 18,574 |

**Mileage at 31/12/50 890,492**
**Lifetime Mileage 1,266,776**
**Withdrawn week ending 26/8/61**
**from Carlisle Upperby**
**Scrapped Crewe Works 9/61**

### REPAIRS

21/12/30-3/1/31**LO** (11)
17/3/32-28/4/32**HS** (36)
19/11/32-9/12/32**LS** (18)
22/2/34-12/4/34**HG** (42)
12/2/35-4/3/35**HS** (18)
16/1/36-19/2/36**HG** (30)
10/2/37-1/3/37**LS** (17)
10/9/37-8/10/37**HG** (25)
13/10/38-15/11/38**HS** (29)
5/1/40-16/2/40**HG** (37)
18/10/41-12/11/41**LS** (22)
17/10/42-7/11/42**HG** (19)
24/2/44-11/3/44**HS** (15)
12/9/45-13/10/45**HS** (28)
24/6/47-13/9/47**HG** (71)
22/9/47-27/9/47**NC Rect** (6)
26/2/49-23/3/49**LI** (22)
29/3/49-13/4/49**NC(Rect)** (14)
15/2/51-21/3/51**HI** (29)
27/3/51-13/4/51**NC(Rect)** (15)
6/2/52-16/5/52**HG** (85)
19/5/52-30/5/52**NC Rect** (10)
3/6/52-19/6/52**NC Rect EO** (14)
20/6/52-5/7/52**NC Rect EO** (13)
30/12/53-2/2/54**HG** (29)
5/2/54-15/2/54**NC (Rect) EO** (8)
8/3/54-29/3/54**NC (Rect) EO** (18)
27/7/55-20/8/55**HI** (21)
24/8/55-24/8/55**NC (Rect) EO** (1)
25/8/55-9/9/55**NC (Rect) EO** (13)
14/9/55-30/9/55**NC (Rect) EO** (14)
3/10/55-15/10/55**NC (Rect) EO** (11)
3/11/56-15/12/56**HG** (36)
25/6/58-20/8/58**LI** (48)
9/12/58-4/2/59**LC(EO)** (47) AWS
GEAR FITTED
9/9/59-30/10/59 **LI** (44)

### TENDERS

| No | Fitted |
|----|--------|
| 4190 | |
| 3190 | 26/12/31 |
| 4511 | 16/5/52 |

5501 ST DUNSTAN'S, the second of the original pair, in a very begrimed red. It carries a 1B Camden shed plate; it was there from late 1935 to early 1937 and again for periods in 1937 to 1939. The engine carried the name SIR FRANK REE at first and this was not replaced (it went to 5530) until March 1937. Given that the vacuum pump is still there and the rain strip has yet to appear, a good guess would be that this picture dates from later that year. Photograph J.T. Rutherford, The Transport Treasury.

45501 at work on BR, heading north past Camden in May 1958. The first two engines had the LNWR arrangement of the left-hand crank leading, against the standard LMS practice of right-hand crank. Presumably they did not reset the wheels on the axles – except the crank axle of course – when they used the old Claughton wheels. It was important to remember when setting them for a Valve & Piston exam, otherwise after dropping the motion on one side, when they were moved, the other sets were in the wrong place. If engines had been stabled behind, oh calamity! Photograph J. Robertson, The Transport Treasury.

# 45502 ROYAL NAVAL DIVISION (from 5/6/37)

**Built Crewe 1/7/32 Replacement for 5959 (LNWR CLAUGHTON No 2426)**
*Renumbered 5959 to 5502  28/5/34*
*5502 to 45502 week ending 20/11/48*

**REPAIRS**
8/3/33-22/3/33**LS** (13)
16/4/34-8/6/34**HG** (37)
11/4/35-7/5/35**HS** (22)
10/12/35-24/12/35**LS** (13)
23/6/36-16/7/36**LS** (21)
27/2/37-10/3/37**HG** (26)
5/5/38-1/6/38**HS** (24)
14/3/39-6/4/39**HS** (21)
30/3/40-29/4/40**HG** (26)
25/8/41-16/9/41**HS** (20)
18/5/43-3/6/43**HG** (15)
15/6/44-30/6/44**LS** (14)
25/9/45-27/10/45**HS** (29)
25/7/47-18/9/47**HG** (48)
23/10/48-19/11/48**HS** (24)
22/5/49-16/6/49**LC** (22)
22/4/50-29/5/50**HG** (31)
10/5/51-29/5/51**LI** (16)
28/5/52-23/6/52**HI** (22)
30/12/53-13/3/54**HG** (63)
23/1/56-25/2/56**HI** (29)
28/7/56-23/8/56**LC(EO)** (22)
10/9/56-14/9/56**LC** (4)
20/8/57-2/10/57**HG** (37)
17/3/59-25/4/59**LI** (33) AWS GEAR FITTED

**SHEDS**
Camden 29/7/33
Longsight 8/6/34
Camden 8/6/34
Edge Hill 8/6/35
Camden 6/7/35
Longsight 23/11/40
Rugby 31/5/41
Willesden 5/6/43
Bushbury 20/5/44
Carlisle Upperby 9/3/46
Carlisle Kingmoor (Loan) 7/9/46
Carlisle Upperby (Loan) 12/10/46
Carlisle Upperby 2/11/46
Preston 16/11/46
Carlisle Upperby 1/10/49
Crewe North 10/6/50
Willesden 29/11/52
Camden 10/1/53
Carlisle Upperby 21/2/53
Preston 21/11/59
Carlisle Upperby 23/4/60

**MILEAGES**
| | |
|---|---|
| 1932 | 44,955 |
| 1933 | 79,789 |
| 1934 | 59,622 |
| 1935 | 71,292 |
| 1936 | 78,859 |
| 1937 | 74,822 |
| 1938 | 73,421 |
| 1939 | 59,656 |
| 1940 | 50,057 |
| 1941 | 48,863 |
| 1942 | 48,792 |
| 1943 | 56,027 |
| 1944 | 47,428 |
| 1945 | 33,692 |
| 1946 | 43,582 |
| 1947 | 36,253 |
| 1948 | 40,268 |
| 1949 | 42,137 |
| 1950 | 41,987 |
| 1951 | 39,806 |
| 1952 | 38,252 |
| 1953 | 38,347 |
| 1954 | 39,840 |
| 1955 | 34.063 |
| 1956 | 37,836 |
| 1957 | 38,521 |
| 1958 | 43,333 |
| 1959 | 32,896 |
| 1960 | 14,199 |

**Mileage at 31/12/50  1,031,502**
**Lifetime Mileage 1,388,595**
**Withdrawn week ending 3/9/60 from Carlisle Upperby - first of class to be withdrawn from service**
**Scrapped Crewe Works 10/60**

**BOILERS**
| Fitted | Number | Received From | When Removed Passed To |
|---|---|---|---|
| 1/7/32 | | | 5510 |
| 10/5/34 | | 5946 | 5910 |
| 24/4/35 | | 5520 | 5544 |
| 15/5/37 | | 5522 | |
| 29/4/40 | 5357 | 5542 | 5514 |
| 3/6/43 | 6033 | 5550 | 5503 |
| 18/9/47 | 5369 | 5538 | 45546 |
| 29/5/50 | 6007 | 45538 | 45506 |
| 13/3/54 | 5976 | 45539 | WDL |
| 2/10/57 | 5483 | 45500 | WDL |

**TENDERS**
| No | Fitted |
|---|---|
| 4474 | 1/7/32 |
| 3190 | 23/6/52 |
| 4488 | 13/3/54 |
| 3904 | 14/9/56 |
| 3909 | 14/9/57 |

45502 started life as 5959. Here it is new in red, with the first type of straight smoke deflectors, flush buffer beam, grab iron on running plate and the other period features – lack of rain strip on cab, crosshead-driven vacuum pump and 'enclosed' cylinder drain cocks. It became 5502 in 1934 and ROYAL NAVAL DIVISION in 1937.

A smart Crewe North Patriot, 45503 THE ROYAL LEICESTERSHIRE REGIMENT in BR green, departs from Crewe for Shrewsbury on 9 May 1954. It was in Crewe Works just over a week later so may have been gently 'pacing itself' before the attention. Photograph B.K.B. Green, Initial Photographics.

# 45503 THE LEICESTERSHIRE REGIMENT (from 8/7/38 and THE ROYAL LEICESTERSHIRE REGIMENT from 3/11/48)

Built Crewe 1/7/32 Replacement for 5985 (LNWR CLAUGHTON No 808)
*Renumbered 5985 to 5503 14/7/34*
*5503 to 45503 week ending 15/5/48*

**TENDERS**

| No | Fitted |
|---|---|
| 4475 | 1/7/32 |
| 4484 | 21/7/34 |
| 4475 | 21/9/34 |
| 4493 | 3/5/58 |
| 4487 | 23/4/59 |

**BOILERS**

| Fitted | | Number Received From | When Removed Passed To |
|---|---|---|---|
| 1/7/32 | | | 6005 |
| 1/2/34 | | 5974 | 5513 |
| 18/12/34 | | 5975 | 5535 |
| 4/11/35 | | 5511 | |
| 13/6/38 | 6171 | 5520 | 5531 |
| 5/6/41 | 5368 | 5533 | 5509 |
| 23/10/45 | 6031 | 5522 | 5519 |
| 10/5/48 | 6033 | 5502 | 45524 |
| 31/1/52 | 5353 | 45506 | 45538 |
| 23/1/57 | 5357 | 45509 | WDL |

**REPAIRS**
1/5/33-24/5/33**LS** (21)
22/1/34-28/2/34**HG** (33)
10/12/34-1/1/35**HS** (19)
22/10/35-13/11/35**HG** (20)
5/10/36-19/10/36**HS** (13)
14/6/37-29/6/37**LS** (14)
6/6/38-30/6/38**HG** (22)
30/11/39-23/12/39**HS** (21)
24/9/40-11/10/40**LS** (16)
12/5/41-5/6/41**HG** (22)
26/10/42-12/11/42**LS** (16)
8/2/44-26/2/44**HS** (17)
6/10/45-23/10/45**HG** (15)
6/1/47-29/1/47**HS** (21)
14/4/48-10/5/48**HG** (23)
9/11/48-15/11/48**NC** (6)
5/5/49-26/5/49**LC** (19)
3/3/50-3/4/50**LI** (26)
26/8/50-25/9/50**LC** (25)
3/12/51-31/1/52**HG** (49)
23/6/53-25/7/53**HI** (28)
18/5/54-15/6/54**LC(EO)** (24)
5/6/55-29/6/55 **HI** (20)
22/11/56-23/1/57**HG** (51)
14/3/58-3/5/58**LI** (42)
11/3/59-23/4/59**LC** (36) AWS GEAR
FITTED
5/3/60-29/4/60**HI** (46)

**SHEDS**
Camden 13/5/33
Crewe North 2/2/35
Edge Hill 20/4/35
Camden 6/7/35
Aston 25/9/37
Preston 11/3/39
Carlisle Upperby 29/7/39
Patricroft 4/10/41
Preston 11/4/42
Edge Hill 9/5/42
Willesden 5/6/43
Camden 8/6/46
Crewe North 18/10/47
Longsight 29/4/50
Crewe North 24/6/50
Carlisle Upperby 22/9/56
Crewe North 3/11/56
Newton Heath 26/7/58
Crewe North 4/10/58
Warrington 4/7/59
Carnforth 18/6/60
Carlisle Upperby 10/9/60

**MILEAGES**

| | |
|---|---|
| 1932 | 39,958 |
| 1933 | 74,112 |
| 1934 | 67,795 |
| 1935 | 64,571 |
| 1936 | 65,906 |
| 1937 | 52,444 |
| 1938 | 48,213 |
| 1939 | 48,280 |
| 1940 | 42,080 |
| 1941 | 38,168 |
| 1942 | 32,071 |
| 1943 | 35,447 |
| 1944 | 36,487 |
| 1945 | 28,086 |
| 1946 | 35,615 |
| 1947 | 44,807 |
| 1948 | 34,368 |
| 1949 | 42,063 |
| 1950 | 38,420 |
| 1951 | 35,014 |
| 1952 | 39,752 |
| 1953 | 38,521 |
| 1954 | 34,155 |
| 1955 | 44,742 |
| 1956 | 37,553 |
| 1957 | 41,547 |
| 1958 | 33,534 |
| 1959 | 33,326 |
| 1960 | 36,127 |
| 1961 | 22,119 |

**Mileage at 31/12/50 868,891**
**Lifetime Mileage 1,265,281**
**Withdrawn week ending 12/8/61**
**from Carlisle Upperby**
**Scrapped Crewe Works 9/61**

After its month in Crewe Works, 45503 (which certainly didn't receive a repaint) was working much further abroad. On 26 August 1954 it was at Carlisle taking water in readiness to take a train back south. 45503 was one of the many Patriot naming peculiarities; it got its first regimental plates, THE LEICESTERSHIRE REGIMENT in 1938 and these were re-cast (presumably to reflect a change in the Regiment's title) at the end of 1948. Photograph J.L. Stevenson.

45504 ROYAL SIGNALS departs Manchester London Road with the 10.50am to Euston, 15 March 1953. Like all the original Patriots by now, the engine carries '6P' on the cab instead of the old '5XP'; the engines, along with the Jubilees, were officially 6P5F from 1955 but continued to carry just the '6P'. Photograph B.K.B. Green, Initial Photographics.

# 45504 ROYAL SIGNALS (from 10/4/37)

**Built Crewe 18/7/32 Replacement for 5987 (LNWR CLAUGHTON No 1096)**
*Renumbered 5987 to 5504 28/6/34*
*5504 to 45504 week ending 2/10/48*

**REPAIRS**
29/5/33-20/6/33**LS** (20)
15/12/33-22/1/34**HG** (32)
29/8/34-3/10/34**HS** (31)
13/8/35-4/9/35**HG** (20)
13/1/37-19/2/37**HG** (33)
18/1/38-31/1/38**HS** (12)
4/1/39-26/1/39**HG** (20)
13/2/40-24/2/40**LS** (11)
14/2/41-13/3/41**HG** (24)
11/9/41-8/11/41**LO** (51)
15/4/43-1/5/43**HS** (15)
8/11/43-24/11/43**LO** (15)
8/3/45-24/3/45**HS** (15)
11/1/47-28/1/47**HG** (15)
25/9/47-17/10/47**NC** (47)
26/8/48-1/10/48**LS** (32)
4/10/48-12/10/48**NC(Rect)** (8)
22/9/49-14/11/49**HG** (46)
7/3/51-29/3/51**HI** (18)
26/11/51-12/1/52**LC** (39)
21/8/52-13/9/52**HI** (20)
13/11/53-18/12/53**HG** (30)
19/10/54-16/11/54**LC** (24)
23/5/55-15/6/55**HI** (20)
13/6/56-20/7/56**HI** (32)
11/3/58-26/4/58**HG** (39)
11/8/59-30/9/59**LI** (43)
1/2/60-28/4/60**HC(EO)** (74)
24/5/60-5/7/60**HC(EO)** (36)
3/2/61-5/4/61**LC(EO)** (51)

**SHEDS**
Preston 22/7/33
Edge Hill 23/9/33
Camden 6/7/35
Camden 20/2/37
Willesden 11/10/41
Camden 5/6/43
Willesden 9/10/43
Camden 3/5/47
Crewe North 11/10/47
Carlisle Upperby 29/1/55
Bristol 15/11/58

**TENDERS**
| No | Fitted |
|---|---|
| 4476 | 18/7/32 |

**BOILERS**

| Fitted | Number Received From | When Removed Passed To |
|---|---|---|
| 18/7/32 | | 5958 |
| 2/1/34 | 5910 | 5511 |
| 21/8/35 | 5551 | 5506 |
| 5/2/37 | 5541 | |
| 26/1/39 | 5352 5534 | 5515 |
| 13/3/41 | 5978 5523 | 5532 |
| 1/3/43 | 6004 5529 | |
| 28/1/47 | 5996 5550 | |
| 14/11/49 | 6008 5540 | 45515 |
| 18/12/53 | 5977 45538 | 45546 |
| 26/4/58 | 6008 45515 | WDL |

**MILEAGES**
| | |
|---|---|
| 1932 | 36,729 |
| 1933 | 66,537 |
| 1934 | 68,874 |
| 1935 | 57,271 |
| 1936 | 73,183 |
| 1937 | 59,475 |
| 1938 | 54,004 |
| 1939 | 58,649 |
| 1940 | 52,586 |
| 1941 | 31,530 |
| 1942 | 49,846 |
| 1943 | 33,419 |
| 1944 | 37,113 |
| 1945 | 41,325 |
| 1946 | 30,007 |
| 1947 | 26,658 |
| 1948 | 34,333 |
| 1949 | 35,881 |
| 1950 | 47,447 |
| 1951 | 37,266 |
| 1952 | 43,168 |
| 1953 | 35,620 |
| 1954 | 37,834 |
| 1955 | 41,957 |
| 1956 | 39,850 |
| 1957 | 31,290 |
| 1958 | 24,451 |

**Mileage at 31/12/50 894,867 presumably to 15/11/58 only; 87,723 miles in WR use. Lifetime mileage 1,274,026**
**Withdrawn week ending 17/3/62 from Bristol; broken up at Crewe 23/3/62**
**Scrapped Crewe Works 3/62**

# 45505 THE ROYAL ARMY ORDNANCE CORPS (from 8/47)

**Built Crewe 26/7/32 Replacement for 5949 (LNWR CLAUGHTON No 2450)**
*Renumbered 5949 to 5505 19/6/34*
*5505 to 45505 week ending 26/6/48*

### TENDERS

| No | Fitted |
|---|---|
| 4477 | 26/7/32 |
| 3190 | 9/3/54 |
| 4236 | 5/11/54 |
| 4569 | 2/4/60 (HIGH STRAIGHT SIDED) |

### MILEAGES

| Year | Mileage |
|---|---|
| 1932 | 30,551 |
| 1933 | 60,549 |
| 1934 | 71,105 |
| 1935 | 62,421 |
| 1936 | 74,247 |
| 1937 | 78,387 |
| 1938 | 72,689 |
| 1939 | 47,546 |
| 1940 | 48,158 |
| 1941 | 53,757 |
| 1942 | 43,000 |
| 1943 | 47,202 |
| 1944 | 53,169 |
| 1945 | 40,563 |
| 1946 | 34,498 |
| 1947 | 30,196 |
| 1948 | 39,786 |
| 1949 | 39,009 |
| 1950 | 39,684 |
| 1951 | 36,612 |
| 1952 | 41,664 |
| 1953 | 39,765 |
| 1954 | 36,145 |
| 1955 | 40,645 |
| 1956 | 43,200 |
| 1957 | 34,848 |
| 1958 | 41,379 |
| 1959 | 36,936 |
| 1960 | 25,024 |
| 1961 | 20,123 |

**Mileage at 31/12/50 966,517 Lifetime Mileage Approx 1,365,000**
**Withdrawn week ending 2/6/62 from Lancaster**
**Stored 29/10/61-29/1/62 and 14/5/62 - Withdrawal**
**Scrapped Crewe Works 8/62**

### BOILERS

| Fitted | Number | Received From | When Removed Passed To |
|---|---|---|---|
| 26/7/32 | | | 5507 |
| 31/5/34 | | 5993 | STOCK |
| 11/3/35 | | 5523 | STOCK |
| 28/7/36 | | 5543 | STOCK |
| 12/1/38 | 6010 | 5508 | 5526 |
| 21/3/40 | 5358 | 5514 | |
| 18/3/42 | 6000 | 5545 | 5532 |
| 26/8/44 | 5998 | 5520 | 45549 |
| 23/6/48 | 6177 | 5508 | |
| 2/6/51 | 6175 | 45542 | 45524 |
| 12/9/55 | 5995 | 45516 | 45518 |
| 16/8/57 | 5984 | 45538 | WDL |

### SHEDS

Edge Hill 14/8/32
Crewe North 7/9/32
Edge Hill 20/4/35
Camden 6/7/35
Rugby 9/11/35
Camden 16/11/35
Willesden 11/10/41
Camden 5/6/43
Carlisle Upperby 11/1/47
Preston 11/10/47
Carlisle Upperby 1/10/49
Preston 7/7/51
Carlisle Upperby 15/9/51
Preston 12/6/54
Longsight 18/9/54
Carlisle Upperby 10/9/60
Lancaster 10/2/62

### REPAIRS

24/5/33-27/5/33**LO** (4)
6/6/33-28/6/33**LS** (20)
28/5/34-19/6/34**HG** (25)
5/9/34-28/9/34**LO** (21)
25/2/35-20/3/35**HS** (21)
14/11/35-2/12/35**LS** (16)
23/6/36-11/8/36**HG** (43)
4/1/38-20/1/38**HS** (15)
16/1/39-7/2/39**LS** (20)
19/2/40-21/3/40**HG** (28)
19/4/40-7/5/40**LO** (16)
25/4/41-14/5/41**HS** (17)
3/2/42-18/3/42**HS** (38)
13/4/43-1/5/43**LS** (17)
18/11/43-18/12/43**LS** (18)
9/8/44-26/8/44**HG** (16)
15/10/45-15/11/45**LS** (28)
13/5/46-12/6/46**LO** (27)
17/10/46-21/11/46**LO** (31)
4/8/47-3/9/37**HS** (27)
4/11/47-5/12/47**LO** (28)
21/1/48-11/2/48**TRO** (19)
6/5/48-23/6/48**HG** (42)
25/8/49-27/9/49**LI** (29)
21/4/51-2/6/51**HG** (36)
6/9/52-27/9/52**HI** (18)
15/2/54-9/3/54**HI** (19)
27/10/54-24/11/54**LC(EO)** (24)
5/8/55-12/9/55**HG** (32)
7/5/56-16/6/56**LC** (35)
7/9/56-15/9/56**NC(EO)** (7)
12/6/57-16/8/57**HG** (56)
5/9/57-21/9/57**NC(Rect)EO** (14)
23/1/59-27/2/59**LI** (30) AWS GEAR FITTED
25/1/60-2/4/60**HI** (59)
18/6/60-12/8/60**LC(EO)** (47)
1/3/61-17/4/61**LC(EO)** (39)
18/9/61-19/10/61**HC(EO)** (27)

45504 ROYAL SIGNALS readies to leave Birmingham New Street platform 7 with the 2.15pm Bristol-York, 11 July 1959. It was of course on this web of cross country work that the so-called 'Second Division' came to the fore. Photograph Michael Mensing.

*Left.* 45505 THE ROYAL ARMY ORDNANCE CORPS stands at the east end of Platform 9, Birmingham New Street on 1 March 1958, ready to take over the northbound Pines Express. It had arrived at Birmingham just before noon on a train from Liverpool and Manchester and crossed to the Midland side of the station for this return working facing the same direction. Photograph Michael Mensing.

*Below.* Sadder times with 45505 THE ROYAL ARMY ORDNANCE CORPS at Lancaster Green Ayre shed, 17 March 1962. It had arrived from Upperby a few weeks before, together with three other Patriots, to see out their last few months on Morecambe-Leeds trains and suchlike. AWS has appeared by now, along with a plain, high sided tender. Photograph Collection Paul Chancellor.

# 45506 THE ROYAL PIONEER CORPS (from 15/9/48)

Built Crewe 1/8/32 Replacement for 5974 (LNNR CLAUGHTON No 1747)
*Renumbered 5974 to 5506 14/7/34*
*5506 to 45506 week ending 4/9/48*

### TENDERS

| No | Fitted |
|----|--------|
| 4478 | 1/8/32 |

### REPAIRS

25/4/33-17/5/33**LS** (20)
9/10/33-9/11/33**HG** (28)
15/12/33-23/12/33**LO** (8)
22/10/34-15/11/34**HS** (22)
18/6/35-11/7/35**LS** (21)
25/1/36-25/2/36**HG** (27)
22/2/37-16/3/37**HS** (20)
9/6/38-2/8/38**HG** (47)
6/2/40-8/3/40**LS** (28)
17/4/42-20/5/42**HG** (29)
12/1/44-27/1/44**LS** (14)
24/9/45-11/10/45**HG**(16)
28/10/46-16/11/46**LS** (18)
5/12/46-28/12/46**LO** (20)
17/7/48-31/8/48**HS** (39)
2/2/50-1/3/50**HI** (23)
28/9/51-14/11/51**HG** (40)
16/2/53-7/3/53**HI** (17)
20/7/53-3/8/53**LC(EO)** (12)
17/11/54-20/12/54**HG** (28)
2/4/56-2/6/56**HI** (53)
7/10/56-22/10/56**NC(EO)** (12)
27/11/56-16/1/57**HC** (41)
13/4/58-2/6/58**HG** (42)
3/8/59-30/9/59**LI** (50)
8/10/59-12/11/59**LC(EO)** (30)
5/5/60-28/6/60**LC(EO)** (44)
26/10/60-25/1/61**LC(EO)** (76)

### BOILERS

| Fitted | | Number Received From | When Removed Passed To |
|--------|---|------|------|
| 1/8/32 | | | STOCK |
| 25/10/33 | | 5982 | STOCK |
| 5/11/34 | | 6029 | STOCK |
| 10/2/36 | | 5537 | STOCK |
| 4/3/37 | 6178 | 5504 | STOCK |
| 14/7/38 | 6170 | 5505 | 5540 |
| 20/5/42 | 6173 | 5516 | 5512 |
| 11/10/45 | 6006 | 5523 | |
| 31/8/48 | 5353 | 5515 | 45502 |
| 14/11/51 | 6170 | 45519 | |
| 20/12/54 | 6007 | 45502 | 45519 |
| 2/6/58 | 5998 | 45537 | WDL |

### SHEDS

Camden 14/8/32
Bushbury 20/4/35
Camden 25/7/36
Willesden 10/6/39
Rugby 23/11/40
Willesden 5/6/43
Edge Hill 16/6/45
Longsight 25/1/47
Preston 5/4/47
Carlisle Upperby 21/6/47
Crewe North 28/5/49
Willesden 5/7/52
Crewe North 20/9/52
Carlisle Upperby 29/1/55
Bristol 15/11/58

### MILEAGES

| Year | Mileage |
|------|---------|
| 1932 | 41,077 |
| 1933 | 67,623 |
| 1934 | 69,671 |
| 1935 | 62,188 |
| 1936 | 58,058 |
| 1937 | 70,153 |
| 1938 | 51,795 |
| 1939 | 64,747 |
| 1940 | 38,078 |
| 1941 | 43,068 |
| 1942 | 35,404 |
| 1943 | 35,069 |
| 1944 | 31,485 |
| 1945 | 33,932 |
| 1946 | 33,250 |
| 1947 | 38,910 |
| 1948 | 31,739 |
| 1949 | 35,817 |
| 1950 | 40,599 |
| 1951 | 30,034 |
| 1952 | 45,848 |
| 1953 | 37,668 |
| 1954 | 38,193 |
| 1955 | 40,783 |
| 1956 | 29,010 |
| 1957 | 40,885 |
| 1958 | 33,843 |

**Presumably to 15/11/58 only**
**Mileage at 31/12/50 882,663 plus**
**107,915 15/11/58 to 17/3/62**
**Lifetime Mileage 1,286,842**
**Withdrawn week ending 17/3/62**
**from Bristol**
**Scrapped Crewe Works 3/62**

45506 THE ROYAL PIONEER CORPS, bright in BR green, at Crewe North shed, 8 August 1953. There was nothing quite like that Patriot chimney, perched above that vast flat bottomed Midland style smokebox. Photograph A.G. Ellis, The Transport Treasury.

While it should not be said that the Patriots were exactly parochial, they could not be found so widely as the other 4-6-0 passenger engines, the Royal Scots and the Jubilees. The latter two types were spread across the Western, Midland and Northern Divisions with the Jubilees additionally and permanently present in the Central Division. The Patriots the other hand were poorly represented in the Midland Division and though many went there at first they were removed after a couple of years and effectively never went back. There was 5509 at Derby for many years and three stalwarts remained at Bristol until withdrawal but that was about it. They were largely absent from Scotland though Polmadie had three for some years in the 1930s. They were more or less unheard of beyond Glasgow and only a handful were ever based in the Central Division, and then only really towards the end. So it's impossible to resist 45506 on 18 May 1961 at Eastleigh, of all places, having arrived there in almost inconceivable circumstances – working a Bromford Bridge-Fawley oil train, of all things. A Lord Nelson just manages to peep through. Photograph Les Elsey.

# 45507 ROYAL TANK CORPS (from 20/11/37)

**Built Crewe 12/8/32 Replacement for 5936 (LNWR CLAUGHTON No 1334)**
*Renumbered 5936 to 5507 23/7/34*
*        5507 to 45507 week ending 23/10/48*

**TENDERS**

| No | Fitted |
|---|---|
| 4480 | 12/8/32 |
| 4473 | 15/10/54 |
| 4248 | 15/5/59 |

**BOILERS**

| Fitted | Number | Received From | When Removed Passed To |
|---|---|---|---|
| 12/8/32 | | | 5532 |
| 28/6/34 | | 5505 | 5508 |
| 1/10/35 | | 5546 | STOCK |
| 16/9/36 | | 5957 | STOCK |
| 12/7/38 | 5365 | 5525 | 5518 |
| 6/1/40 | 6177 | 5550 | 5508 |
| 10/9/43 | 6003 | 5514 | 5517 |
| 5/1/46 | 6012 | 5551 | 45541 |
| 8/8/51 | 6029 | 45518 | |
| 9/8/56 | 6169 | 45511 | 45509 |
| 15/5/59 | 5988 | 45533 | WDL |

**MILEAGES**

| Year | Mileage |
|---|---|
| 1932 | 26,261 |
| 1933 | 72,640 |
| 1934 | 68,802 |
| 1935 | 65,207 |
| 1936 | 56,976 |
| 1937 | 61,867 |
| 1938 | 53,710 |
| 1939 | 46,151 |
| 1940 | 32,863 |
| 1941 | 41,502 |
| 1942 | 44,076 |
| 1943 | 55,841 |
| 1944 | 45,598 |
| 1945 | 39,210 |
| 1946 | 45,505 |
| 1947 | 25,001 |
| 1948 | 30,255 |
| 1949 | 44,027 |
| 1950 | 34,930 |
| 1951 | 35,506 |
| 1952 | 41,846 |
| 1953 | 41,685 |
| 1954 | 44,585 |
| 1955 | 42,204 |
| 1956 | 37,004 |
| 1957 | 42,150 |
| 1958 | 41,177 |
| 1959 | 35,221 |
| 1960 | 29,148 |

**Mileage at 31/12/50 890,422**
**Withdrawn week ending 20/10/62**
**from Lancaster**
**Stored 29/10/61-29/1/62 and**
**28/5/62 - withdrawal**
**Scrapped Horwich Works 3/63**

**REPAIRS**
8/5/33-9/5/33**LO** (2)
12/6/33-30/6/33**LS** (17)
11/6/34-23/7/34**HG** (37)
12/3/35-29/3/35**HS** (16)
25/9/35-8/10/35**HO** (12)
8/9/36-2/10/36**HG** (22)
30/8/37-23/9/37**HS** (22)
20/1/38-28/1/38**LO** (8)
16/6/38-28/7/38**HG** (37)
9/12/39-6/1/40**HS** (24)
10/11/41-28/11/41**LS** (17)
24/8/43-10/9/43**HG** (16)
21/10/44-3/11/44**HS** (12)
21/11/45-5/1/46**HG** (39)
23/6/47-5/8/47**LS** (38)
6/1/48-31/1/48**LO** (23)
12/9/48-21/10/48**LO** (34)
10/5/49-26/5/49**LI** (15)
29/6/50-24/8/50**LC** (48)
22/6/51-8/8/51**HG** (40)
25/2/53-24/3/53**HI** (23)
30/4/54-31/5/54**HI** (26)
9/6/56-9/8/56**HG** (52)
21/1/58-15/2/58**LI** (22)
21/3/59-15/5/59**HC** (46) AWS
GEAR FITTED
30/3/60-8/6/60**LC(EO)** (59)
10/4/61-9/5/61**LI** (25)

**SHEDS**
Crewe 12/8/32
Longsight 6/10/34
Leeds 1/12/34
Camden 6/4/35
Bushbury 20/4/35
Bescot 25/9/37
Crewe North 11/3/39
Rugby 28/10/39
Willesden 5/6/43
Camden 2/10/43
Crewe North 18/10/47
Preston (Loan) 5/2/49
Crewe North 26/2/49
Carlisle Upperby 20/9/58
Preston 21/11/59
Carlisle Upperby 9/1/60
Lancaster 10/2/62

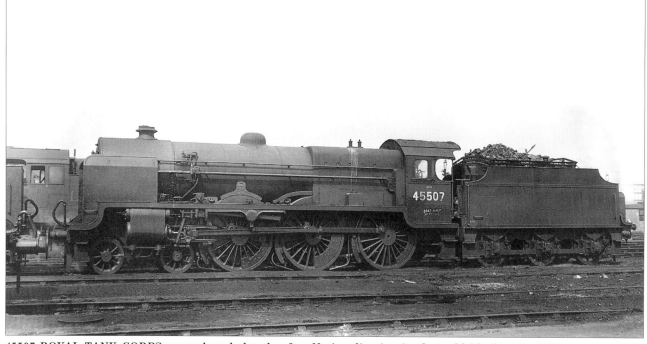

45507 ROYAL TANK CORPS renumbered shortly after Nationalisation in that odd block style; LMS so covered in muck as to be untraceable. Four bolt holes on crosshead bracket *in memoriam* of the removed vacuum pump; it probably won't be possible to see this on the print as published but the middle driving wheel has the 'webbing' on the four spokes off the crank pin; the other two drivers don't. Note ex-Claughton reverser handwheel to be seen through the cab window. This is Crewe North; chalked on the cab is BARS WANT SETTING – presumably referring to the firebars. Photograph W. Hermiston, The Transport Treasury.

Late detail on a Patriot. 45507 ROYAL TANK CORPS has the various final additions – in the first instance AWS, at Kentish Town on 1 July 1959, an odd place to find an Upperby engine and secondly with electrification flashes at Crewe South, in 1961. At this late date it has a nicely blacked smokebox door and painted number plate, though the rest of it looks pretty rough.

# 45508

**Built Crewe 9/8/32 Replacement for 6010**
**(LNWR CLAUGHTON No 149)**
*Renumbered 6010 to 5508 17/4/34*
*5508 to 45508 week ending 8/1/49*

**BOILERS**

| Fitted | Number | Received From | When Removed Passed To |
|---|---|---|---|
| 9/8/32 | | | STOCK |
| 28/3/34 | | 6023 | STOCK |
| 8/11/35 | | 5507 | 5518 |
| 12/3/37 | | 6013 | STOCK |
| 28/9/37 | 6173 | 5999 | 5516 |
| 9/5/39 | 5975 | 5539 | 5537 |
| 11/4/41 | 5483 | 5551 | 5527 |
| 18/2/44 | 6177 | 5507 | 45505 |
| 6/9/47 | 5994 | 5525 | 45513 |
| 27/2/50 | 6005 | 5550 | |
| 7/7/53 | 6003 | 45551 | 45541 |
| 7/12/56 | 5986 | 45549 | |
| 21/11/58 | 5999 | 45519 | 45547 |

**REPAIRS**
28/4/33-17/5/33**LS** (17)
23/2/34-17/4/34**HG** (45)
7/1/35-22/1/35**LO** (14)
1/3/35-22/3/35**HS** (19)
31/10/35-18/11/35**HO** (16)
17/4/36-18/5/36**LS** (27)
27/2/37-25/3/37**HG** (23)
6/9/37-6/10/37**HO** (27)
26/4/38-12/5/38**HS** (15)
19/4/39-9/5/39**HG** (18)
20/5/40-4/6/40**LS** (14)
24/3/41-11/4/41**HS** (17)
23/1/42-20/2/42**HS** (25)
12/12/42-23/1/43**LS** (36)
31/1/44-18/2/44**HG** (17)
5/6/45-20/7/45**HS** (40)
27/7/46-29/8/46**HS** (29)
3/7/47-6/9/47**HG** (57)
8/12/48-6/1/49**LI** (25)
10/1/49-17/1/49**NC(Rect)** (7)
16/11/49-7/12/49**LC** (19)
23/1/50-27/2/50**HG** (30)
10/1/51-29/1/51**LC** (16)
20/3/51-14/4/51**LC** (21)
19/4/51-30/4/51**NC(Rect)** (9)
3/1/52-12/2/52**LI** (34)
4/6/53-7/7/53**HG** (28)
27/7/53-15/8/53**LC(EO)** (17)
11/12/54-13/1/55**LI** (26)
26/4/56-24/5/56**LC(EO)** (24)
27/8/56-1/9/56**NC(EO)** (5)
3/11/56-7/12/56**HG** (29) FITTED
WITH STOVE PIPE CHIMNEY,
NOT MENTIONED ON CARD
5/2/57-1/3/57**NC(Rect)(EO)** (21)
17/10/58-21/11/58**HG** (30)
5/10/59-27/10/59**NC(EO)** (19)
AWS GEAR FITTED

**MILEAGES**

| | |
|---|---|
| 1932 | 36,948 |
| 1933 | 85,522 |
| 1934 | 69,769 |
| 1935 | 46,116 |
| 1936 | 59,759 |
| 1937 | 58,313 |
| 1938 | 66,625 |
| 1939 | 62,548 |
| 1940 | 46,855 |
| 1941 | 42,333 |
| 1942 | 40,132 |
| 1943 | 34,249 |
| 1944 | 37,921 |
| 1945 | 37,064 |
| 1946 | 34,290 |
| 1947 | 38,858 |
| 1948 | 36,015 |
| 1949 | 30,815 |
| 1950 | 40,200 |
| 1951 | 35,816 |
| 1952 | 40,372 |
| 1953 | 33,230 |
| 1954 | 36,439 |
| 1955 | 36,282 |
| 1956 | 29,657 |
| 1957 | 43,378 |
| 1958 | 38,566 |
| 1959 | 35,239 |
| 1960 | 26,105 |

**Mileage at 31/12/50 904,332**
**Lifetime Mileage 1,259,416**
**Withdrawn week ending 3/12/60**
**from Carlisle Upperby**
**Scrapped Crewe Works 12/60**

**TENDERS**

| No | Fitted |
|---|---|
| 4479 | 9/8/32 |
| 3922 | 13/1/55 |
| 4488 | 7/12/56 |

**SHEDS**
Crewe North 9/8/32
Longsight 21/10/33
Derby 1/12/34
Camden 16/2/35
Bushbury 4/5/35
Camden 28/8/37
Longsight 23/8/41
Rugby 16/5/42
Willesden 30/4/43
Camden 5/6/43
Willesden 2/10/43
Camden 18/3/44
Edge Hill 17/6/44
Crewe North 30/11/46
Carlisle Upperby 24/7/48
Preston 19/2/49
Carlisle Upperby 9/51
Preston 12/6/54
Longsight 18/9/54
Preston 2/10/54
Carlisle Upperby 1/9/56
Preston 21/11/59
Carlisle Upperby 23/4/60

**5508, an original Patriot in the LMS 1946 livery; bolt holes reveal position of removed vacuum pump. Note the severe dent in the boiler handrail. Photograph J. Robertson, The Transport Treasury.**

# 45509 THE DERBYSHIRE YEOMANRY (from 10/11/51)

**Built Crewe 19/8/32 Replacement for 6005 (LNWR CLAUGHTON No 63)**
*Renumbered 6005 to 5509 10/8/34*
*5509 to 45509 week ending 17/9/49*

## MILEAGES

| Year | Mileage |
|------|---------|
| 1932 | 26,735 |
| 1933 | 74,049 |
| 1934 | 68,867 |
| 1935 | 54,159 |
| 1936 | 53,306 |
| 1937 | 57,143 |
| 1938 | 63,679 |
| 1939 | 59,151 |
| 1940 | 38,296 |
| 1941 | 44,480 |
| 1942 | 47,588 |
| 1943 | 41,661 |
| 1944 | 34,666 |
| 1945 | 18,166 |
| 1946 | 37,023 |
| 1947 | 32,125 |
| 1948 | 35,819 |
| 1949 | 30,965 |
| 1950 | 38,202 |
| 1951 | 37,732 |
| 1952 | 37,701 |
| 1953 | 43,241 |
| 1954 | 44,184 |
| 1955 | 41,284 |
| 1956 | 33,128 |
| 1957 | 43,317 |
| 1958 | 38,304 |
| 1959 | 23,083 |
| 1960 | 35,518 |
| 1961 | 16,280 |

**Mileage at 31/12/50 856,080**
**Lifetime mileage 1,249,852**
**Withdrawn week ending 12/8/61**
**from Newton Heath**
**Scrapped Crewe Works 9/61**

## BOILERS

| Fitted | Number | Received From | When Removed Passed To |
|--------|--------|---------------|------------------------|
| 19/8/32 | | | 6005 |
| 21/2/34 | | 5985 | STOCK |
| 5/6/35 | | 5538 | 5513 |
| 2/3/37 | | 5533 | |
| 27/3/39 | 6004 | 5504 | 5529 |
| 6/9/41 | 5360 | 6017 | |
| 24/11/45 | 5368 | 5503 | |
| 14/9/49 | 6001 | 45540 | 45510 |
| 1/6/54 | 5357 | 45501 | 45503 |
| 30/10/56 | 6032 | 45551 | 45510 |
| 29/12/59 | 6169 | 45507 | WDL |

## SHEDS

Crewe North 28/8/32
Longsight 4/11/33
Derby 1/12/34
Camden 16/2/35
Willesden 9/5/36 Damaged by
enemy action at Willesden on
11/10/40
Longsight 23/8/41
Rugby 16/5/42
Camden 5/6/43
Edge Hill 3/5/47
Willesden 21/6/47
Crewe North (Loan) 9/6/51
Crewe North 28/7/51
Derby (Loan) 20/10/51
Derby 10/11/51
Newton Heath (Loan) 30/8/58
Newton Heath 3/1/59

## REPAIRS

24/7/33-18/8/33**LS** (17)
29/1/34-12/3/34**HG** (37)
15/11/34-4/12/34**LS** (17)
28/5/35-21/6/35**HG** (22)
27/2/37-16/3/37**HG** (20)
28/2/39-27/3/39**HS** (24)
8/6/40-24/6/40**LS** (14)
23/8/41-6/9/41**HG** (13)
26/2/42-21/3/42**LO** (21)
8/9/42-20/10/42**LS** (37)
7/3/44-21/3/44**HS** (13)
31/7/44-26/8/44**LO** (24)
31/10/45-24/11/45**HG** (22)
29/3/46-2/5/46**LO** (29)
24/9/47-31/10/47**HS** (33)
9/8/49-14/9/49**HG** (32)
3/4/51-28/4/51**LI** (22)
3/1/53-27/1/53**HI** (20)
27/4/54-1/6/54**HG** (30)
4/8/55-3/9/55**HI** (26)
7/9/56-30/10/56**HG** (45)
28/3/58-30/4/58**LI** (27)
31/10/59-29/12/59**HG** (48)

## TENDERS

| No | Fitted |
|------|---------|
| 4481 | 19/8/32 |

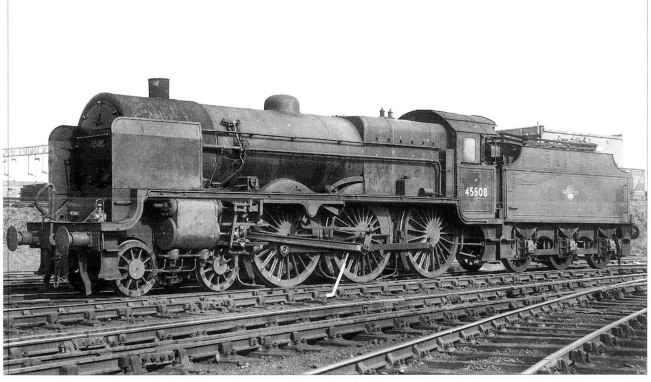

45508, in BR green but with that hideous 'spout', at Crewe South. This draughting had appeared in 1956 but even if it proved to be efficacious it was clear that the days of the original Patriots were hardly stretching endlessly into the future.

5509, bearing what would be the remnants of LMS 'red', at Derby about 1948. What is peculiar is that the engine has still not received the extra cab rain strips. That's the Derby No.4 roundhouse beyond. Photograph W. Hermiston, The Transport Treasury.

45509, now with its cab rain strip, on the 3.35pm St Pancras train, at Derby Midland during its years (most of the 1950s in fact) as a 17A Derby engine. This was a 'returnee' to the Midland Division though it had not gone there from new, merely spending a couple of months at Derby in 1934-35. Photograph M.N. Bland, The Transport Treasury.

# 45510

**Built Crewe 24/8/32 Replacement for 6012 (LNWR CLAUGHTON No 152)**
*Renumbered 6012 to 5510 25/6/34*
*5510 to 45510 week ending 26/6/48*

### SHEDS
Allocated to Midland Division
from new until - 30/10/33
Carlisle Upperby 30/10/33
Leeds 3/11/34
Camden 6/4/35
Crewe North 28/8/35
Camden 28/9/35
Longsight 23/8/41
Rugby 16/5/42
Willesden 5/6/43
Edge Hill 3/5/47
Willesden 21/6/47
Crewe North 28/5/49
Edge Hill 10/2/51
Crewe North 24/3/51
Willesden 5/7/52
Crewe North 20/9/52
Willesden 29/1/55
Carnforth 3/10/59
Carlisle Upperby 10/9/60
Lancaster 10/2/62

### REPAIRS
28/6/33-1/8/33**HS** (30)
2/9/33-23/10/33**HO** (44)
24/5/34-25/6/34**HG** (28)
10/8/35-28/8/35**HS** (16)
26/11/35-6/1/36**HO** (35)
6/12/36-27/1/37**HG** (44)
11/8/37-24/8/37**LS** (12)
18/1/38-28/2/38**HS** (36)
24/2/39-23/3/39**LS** (24)
19/2/40-7/3/40**HG** (16)
7/5/41-24/5/41**LS** (16)
21/2/42-11/4/42**HG** (43)
3/11/42-12/12/42**LO** (35)
18/11/43-23/12/43**LS** (31)
22/1/45-24/2/45**HS** (30)
29/9/46-21/10/46**HG** (19)
5/6/48-23/6/48**LS** (16)
20/3/50-27/4/50**HG** (32)
23/10/51-17/11/51**HI** (22)
13/1/53-21/2/53**HG** (34)
24/2/53-25/2/53**NC Rect** (1)
25/11/54-20/12/54**HG** (21)
4/4/56-18/5/56**HI** (38)
26/6/56-3/7/56**NC(Rect)(EO)** (6)
24/7/57-7/9/57**HI** (39)
30/8/58-3/10/58**HC** (29)
5/3/59-17/4/59**HI** (36) AWS GEAR FITTED
31/5/60-21/7/60**HG** (44)
29/4/61-17/6/61**HC(EO)** (42)

### MILEAGES
| | |
|---|---|
| 1932 | 24,641 |
| 1933 | 62,417 |
| 1934 | 78,572 |
| 1935 | 57,542 |
| 1936 | 75,571 |
| 1937 | 67,756 |
| 1938 | 69,686 |
| 1939 | 56,218 |
| 1940 | 48,228 |
| 1941 | 50,820 |
| 1942 | 35,694 |
| 1943 | 42,269 |
| 1944 | 37,873 |
| 1945 | 36,688 |
| 1946 | 30,050 |
| 1947 | 37,124 |
| 1948 | 30,147 |
| 1949 | 37,659 |
| 1950 | 43,120 |
| 1951 | 38,563 |
| 1952 | 43,075 |
| 1953 | 40,122 |
| 1954 | 34,159 |
| 1955 | 43,685 |
| 1956 | 35,827 |
| 1957 | 40,927 |
| 1958 | 33,444 |
| 1959 | 35,670 |
| 1960 | 33,475 |

**Mileage at 31/12/50 922,075**
**Withdrawn week ending 9/6/62 from Lancaster**
**Stored 29/10/61-29/1/62 and 14/5/62 - withdrawal**
**Scrapped Crewe Works 8/62**

### BOILERS
| Fitted | Number | Received From | When Removed Passed To |
|---|---|---|---|
| 24/8/32 | | | 5521 |
| 10/6/34 | | 5959 | STOCK |
| 19/8/35 | | 5910 | 5524 |
| 12/1/37 | | 5532 | STOCK |
| 21/2/38 | 6031 | 5548 | 5510 |
| 7/3/40 | 5371 | 5530 | |
| 11/4/42 | 6029 | 5529 | 5518 |
| 21/10/46 | 5995 | 5517 | 45516 |
| 27/4/50 | 5976 | 45544 | 45539 |
| 21/2/53 | 6172 | 45537 | 45518 |
| 20/12/54 | 6001 | 45509 | 45544 |
| 21/7/60 | 6032 | 45509 | WDL |

### TENDERS
| No | Fitted |
|---|---|
| 4482 | 24/8/32 |
| 4505 | 13/5/61 |

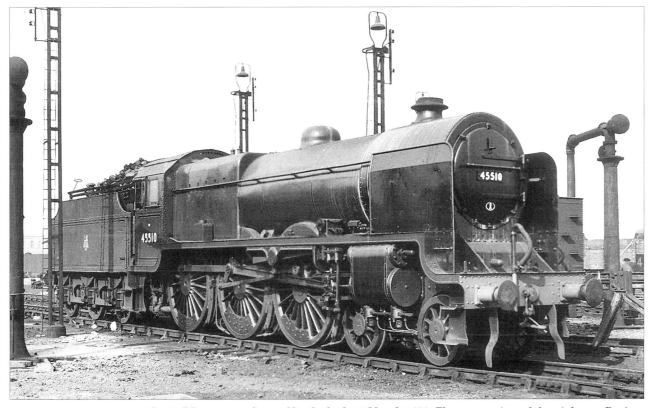

45510 – it was never named – in BR green at Crewe North shed, 15 March 1953. The conversion of the eighteen Pariots left the rest a minor, obsolescent, class of just thirty-four engines, spread the length of the old LNW with a few more far flung examples, so it is hardly surprising that the 'Baby Scots' – despite the wonderful noise thy made – became somewhat 'anonymous' as the 1950s wore on. Nevertheless they could still put on a show – no less than *six* passed Roade during the afternoon of Friday 31 July 1959 for instance! Photograph B.K.B. Green, Initial Photographics.

The better sort of freight was becoming the best the Baby Scots could hope for as the 1950s drew on; 45510 had been at Willesden, a freight shed in the main, for several years by the time of this photograph. On 29 April 1958 it is gathering speed on the way north out of Rugby, on the Trent Valley line with a down fitted freight. Photograph Michael Mensing.

# 45511 ISLE OF MAN (from 1938)

**Built Crewe 31/8/32 Replacement for 5942 (LNWR CLAUGHTON No 2366)**
*Renumbered 5942 to 5511 3/8/34*
*5511 to 45511 week ending 21/5/49*

## REPAIRS
17/7/33-9/8/33**LS** (21)
25/6/34-3/8/34**HG** (35)
26/3/35-7/5/35**HO** (36)
5/9/35-23/9/35**HS** (16)
30/3/36-7/5/36**HG** (33)
15/2/37-5/3/37**HS** (17)
29/12/37-20/1/38**HG** (20)
5/11/38-24/11/38**HS** (17)
30/10/39-18/11/39**HS** (18)
23/10/40-26/11/40**HG** (30)
23/10/41-8/11/41**LS** (15)
23/2/43-12/3/43**HS** (16)
30/5/44-14/6/44**HS** (14)
11/6/45-28/6/45**HS** (16)
13/3/46-30/3/46**LO** (16)
29/8/47-2/10/47**HG** (30)
20/11/47-6/12/47**LO** (15)
29/4/49-19/5/49**LI** (18)
5/10/50-13/11/50**HG** (33)
26/11/51-24/12/51**LI** (24)
17/1/53-5/2/53**LI** (16)
5/10/53-28/10/53**LC** (20)
1/2/54-11/3/54**LC(EO)** (33)
24/1/55-3/3/55**HI** (33)
12/4/56-2/6/56**HG** (44)
6/6/56-25/6/56**NC(Rect)EO** (16)
27/6/56-17/7/56**NC(Rect)EO** (17)
27/1/58-22/2/58**HI** (23)
17/10/58-28/11/58**LC(EO)** (36)
17/9/59-30/10/59**HI** (37) AWS GEAR FITTED
30/8/60-2/9/60**LC(TO)** (3)

## TENDERS
| No | Fitted |
|----|--------|
| 4483 | 31/8/32 |
| 3931 | 10/10/53 |
| 3937 | 3/3/55 |
| 3933 | 22/2/58 |
| 4252 | 2/9/60 |

## BOILERS
| Fitted | Number | Received From | When Removed Passed To |
|--------|--------|---------------|------------------------|
| 31/8/32 | | | 5533 |
| 17/7/34 | | 5962 | STOCK |
| 16/9/35 | | 5504 | STOCK |
| 24/4/36 | | 5962 | 5523 |
| 26/2/37 | 5371 | 5999 | 5530 |
| 5/1/38 | 5359 | 5908 | 5531 |
| 24/11/38 | 5369 | 5540 | 5533 |
| 26/11/40 | 5987 | 5547 | 5512 |
| 12/3/43 | 6169 | 5536 | |
| 2/10/47 | 5984 | 5529 | 5538 |
| 13/11/50 | 6169 | 45511 | 45507 |
| 2/6/56 | 5982 | 45546 | WDL |

## SHEDS
Crewe North 31/8/32
Longsight 11/8/34
Bristol 1/12/34
Edge Hill 20/4/35
Camden 6/7/35
Edge Hill 5/10/35
Camden 2/12/39
Longsight 23/8/41
Crewe North 18/7/42
Bushbury 5/6/43
Crewe North 9/3/46
Edge Hill 24/1/48
Crewe North 14/2/48
Edge Hill (Loan) 28/8/48
Crewe North 13/11/48
Carlisle Upperby 29/4/50
Crewe North 24/6/50
Edge Hill (Loan) 31/3/51
Crewe North 7/4/51
Willesden 28/7/51
Carnforth 17/10/59
Mold Jct 23/1/60
Warrington 23/4/60
Carlisle Upperby 10/9/60

## MILEAGES
| | |
|---|---|
| 1932 | 25,135 |
| 1933 | 73,347 |
| 1934 | 65,301 |
| 1935 | 55,497 |
| 1936 | 57,423 |
| 1937 | 62,517 |
| 1938 | 60,283 |
| 1939 | 61,768 |
| 1940 | 50,414 |
| 1941 | 54,886 |
| 1942 | 43,731 |
| 1943 | 41,438 |
| 1944 | 51,329 |
| 1945 | 32,727 |
| 1946 | 38,816 |
| 1947 | 32,192 |
| 1948 | 46,200 |
| 1949 | 43,149 |
| 1950 | 37,275 |
| 1951 | 38,409 |
| 1952 | 35,083 |
| 1953 | 35,022 |
| 1954 | 29,912 |
| 1955 | 34,506 |
| 1956 | 36,534 |
| 1957 | 44,673 |
| 1958 | 33,305 |
| 1959 | 34,848 |
| 1960 | 25,393 to 30 August |

**Mileage at 31/12/50 933,428 Lifetime**
**Mileage 1,290,459**
**Withdrawn week ending 11/2/61 from Carlisle Upperby**
**Scrapped Crewe Works 3/61**

45511 ISLE OF MAN at Willesden in August 1959. It was notable really for its three legged badge, which often drew amused comment from the platform oiks, safe in our ignorance. The cab 'extension' at the front on this side was to accommodate the ex-Claughton reverser. Photograph R.C. Riley, The Transport Treasury.

45511 at Willesden in October 1958, a photograph first used in *British Railways Illustrated's* first *Annual* of 1992. ISLE OF MAN had languished there for some time, filthy with a leaky smokebox (though it would see further service – theoretically – at three more sheds) when the call came, puzzlingly, to have it photographed for posterity. At least these were the days when a nameplate could be left on a dead locomotive! Poor old 45511 was duly dragged out and *only this side* cleaned. Beware – the camera *does* lie!

5512 BUNSEN at Camden (that famous footbridge and a non-streamlined Pacific beyond) on 14 March 1944. This was a wartime news picture, captioned for official distribution at the time thus: *'A critical period is now approaching – vast allied armies are assembling in Britain: armies that will soon surge into the attack. Wherever and whenever the great attack is launched, the railways will be asked for a tremendous intense effort, greater than that of before. The men of the iron road will be ready, ready to play their part in storming the fortress of Europe.'*

BUNSEN was converted to taper boiler form in 1948; running without smoke deflectors a few weeks later at Northchurch just north of Berkhamsted on 19 August 1948, this is the LMS post-war black, lined straw and maroon, but with BR markings (BR black came in later that year). Photograph H.C. Casserley.

BUNSEN in BR green and with deflectors, at Upperby in April 1957. It was named after the great German chemist but few of us associated it so; how could you name a locomotive after a humble laboratory burner? Some of us assumed it to be a coastal town in Lancashire... Photograph W. Hermiston, The Transport Treasury.

# 45512 BUNSEN

**Built Crewe 14/9/32 Replacement for 5966 (LNWR CLAUGHTON No 1177 BUNSEN)**
*Renumbered 5966 to 5512 14/7/34*
*5512 to 45512 week ending 31/7/48*
*Converted to Class 6P (later 7P) 26/7/48 (10th of 18)*

## MILEAGES

| Year | Mileage |
|---|---|
| 1932 | 25,064 |
| 1933 | 84,585 |
| 1934 | 64,113 |
| 1935 | 70,478 |
| 1936 | 74,706 |
| 1937 | 73,026 |
| 1938 | 77,696 |
| 1939 | 60,542 |
| 1940 | 45,898 |
| 1941 | 54,829 |
| 1942 | 44,586 |
| 1943 | 38,003 |
| 1944 | 53,796 |
| 1945 | 46,208 |
| 1946 | 48,137 |
| 1947 | 50,221 |
| 1948 | 36,616 |
| 1949 | 52,752 |
| 1950 | 56,186 |
| 1951 | 45,665 |
| 1952 | 53,470 |
| 1953 | 47,348 |
| 1954 | 51,633 |
| 1955 | 56,692 |
| 1956 | 54,681 |
| 1957 | 53,901 |
| 1958 | 57,140 |
| 1959 | 56,199 |
| 1960 | 60,806 |

**Mileage at 31/12/50 1,057,442**
**1,594,977 at 31/12/60**
**Withdrawn week ending 27/3/65**
**from Carlisle Kingmoor**
**Scrapped Motherwell Machinery**
**& Scrap Co Wishaw 7/65**

## SHEDS

Camden 14/9/32
Crewe 2/2/35
Edge Hill 20/4/35
Camden 6/7/35
Longsight 26/7/35
Camden 4/1/36
Bushbury (Loan) 20/11/37
Camden 11/12/37
Longsight 23/11/40
Crewe North 18/7/42
Preston 30/1/43
Bushbury 5/6/43
Crewe North 9/3/46

Bushbury 2/10/48
Carlisle Upperby 28/5/49
Carlisle Kingmoor 11/64

## REPAIRS

2/1/34-30/1/34**HG** (25)
10/12/34-28/12/34**HS** (16)
10/7/35-26/7/35**HO** (15)
30/10/35-20/11/35**HG** (19)
27/11/36-4/1/37**HS** (32)
21/11/37-21/12/37**HG** (26)
10/1/38-8/2/38**LO** (26)
14/1/39-15/2/39**HS** (28)
8/4/40-10/5/40**HG** (29)
31/5/41-17/6/41**LS** (15)
29/6/42-12/8/42**HG** (39)
19/11/43-16/12/43**LS** (24)
30/9/44-17/10/44**HS** (15)
2/5/45-17/5/45**TRO** (13)
8/10/45-8/11/45**HG** (28)
21/12/46-9/1/47**LS** (16)

22/4/48-26/7/48**HG** (82)
24/7/50-11/8/50**LI** (16)
20/2/51-21/3/51**LC** (25)
8/5/52-14/6/52**HG** (32) SMOKE DEFLECTORS
FITTED
4/1/54-8/2/54**HI** (30)
21/5/55-7/7/55**HG** (40)
26/6/56-15/8/56**LI** (43)
12/8/57-19/9/57**HG** (33)
17/2/58-29/3/58**LC(EO)** (35)
31/7/58-8/9/58**LI** (33)
7/10/59-27/11/59**LI** (44) AWS GEAR FITTED
10/1/61-8/2/61**HG** (25) SPEEDOMETER
FITTED

## BOILERS

| Fitted | Number From | Received | When Removed Passed To |
|---|---|---|---|
| 14/9/32 | | | 5957 |
| 11/1/34 | | 5948 | STOCK |
| 14/12/34 | | 5506 | STOCK |
| 7/11/35 | | 5519 | |
| 23/12/36 | 5996 | 5515 | 5519 |
| 6/12/37 | 5356 | 5538 | 5551 |
| 10/5/40 | 6031 | 5510 | 5522 |
| 15/8/42 | 5365 | 5518 | |
| 8/11/45 | 6173 | 5506 | 45542 |
| | | | |
| 26/7/48 | 12662 | New | 46115 |
| 14/6/52 | 10752 | 46125 | 46121 |
| 7/7/55 | 12669 | 46155 | 45536 |
| 19/9/57 | 13244 | 45523 | 46156 |
| 8/2/61 | 13242 | 45527 | |

## TENDERS

| No | Fitted |
|---|---|
| 4484 | 14/9/32 |
| 4505 | 7/7/34 |
| 4475 | 21/7/34 |
| 4484 | 21/9/34 |
| | |
| 9759 | 26/7/48 |
| 9342 | 21/1/52 |
| 9759 | 11/3/52 |

45512 BUNSEN, light at Carlisle on 6 December 1956. The Patriots were not allocated to Scotland, though right at the very last BUNSEN made it, in a way, going to Kingmoor for its last months. Kingmoor of course is in England but it had once been a Northern Division shed... Photograph J.L. Stevenson, courtesy Hamish Stevenson.

The end at Kingmoor, with the defiling stripe, 15 May 1965. Photograph J.L. Stevenson, courtesy Hamish Stevenson.

45513 (another one that was never named) pauses at Bletchley with an up slow train on 3 August 1957. Carlisle Upperby engines were always rarities at the south end of the main line. No flyover, no masts or wires, just the open railway with a late surviving LNWR gantry. Photograph Stephen Summerson.

# 45513

**Built Crewe 19/9/32 Replacement for 5958 (LNWR CLAUGHTON No 2416)**
*Renumbered 5958 to 5513 25/7/34*
*5513 to 45513 week ending 12/6/48*

## REPAIRS
5/2/34-22/2/34**HS** (16)
17/3/34-28/3/34**LO** (10)
18/1/35-15/2/35**HG** (25)
19/9/35 30/9/35**LS** (10)
28/1/36-25/2/36**LS** (25)
23/3/37-15/4/37**HG** (20)
27/4/38-13/5/38**LS** (15)
18/2/39-4/4/39**HG** (39)
1/4/40-18/4/40**LS** (16)
17/1/41-4/2/41**LS** (16)
11/9/41-26/9/41**HG** (14)
10/10/41-5/11/41**LS** (23)
20/3/43-9/4/43**HS** (18)
20/10/43-30/10/43**LO** (10)
29/7/44-18/8/44**HS** (18)
31/1/45-10/3/45**LO** (34)
6/10/45-10/11/45**HG** (31)
8/7/47-14/8/47**HS** (32)
21/8/47-27/8/47**NCRect** (6)
6/5/48-12/6/48**HS** (33)
6/1/49-9/3/49**HG** (54)
21/10/49-19/11/49**HC** (26)
11/9/50-5/10/50**LI** (21)
21/7/51-11/8/51**LC** (18)
29/2/52-6/5/52**HG** (56)
6/8/53-11/8/53**NC** (4)
9/11/53-3/12/53**LI** (21)
23/8/55-27/9/55**HG** (30)
21/5/57-17/6/57**LI** (23)
23/7/57-1/8/57**NC(Rect)EO** (8)
3/12/58-5/2/59**HI** (53) AWS GEAR FITTED
12/8/60-8/10/60**HG** (49)
23/1/61-22/2/61**LC(EO)** (26)

## BOILERS

| Fitted | Number From | Received Passed To | When Removed |
|---|---|---|---|
| 19/9/32 | | | 5927 |
| 13/2/34 | | 5987 | 5522 |
| 30/1/35 | | 5985 | STOCK |
| 1/4/37 | | 5509 | |
| 2/4/39 | 5485 | 5517 | |
| 26/9/41 | 5370 | 5538 | |
| 9/4/43 | 5987 | 5511 | 5535 |
| 10/11/45 | 5975 | 5537 | 45517 |
| 9/3/49 | 6002 | 5533 | 45548 |
| 6/5/52 | 5994 | 45508 | 45546 |
| 27/9/55 | 5993 | 5500 | |
| 8/10/60 | 6033 | 45537 | WDL |

## SHEDS
Kentish Town 19/9/32
Leeds 25/3/33
Kentish Town 30/10/33
Camden 16/2/35
Longsight 14/6/41
Crewe North 18/7/42
Bushbury 5/6/43
Edge Hill 9/3/46
Longsight 25/1/47
Preston 18/10/47
Crewe North 21/1/50
Carlisle Upperby 29/1/55
Carnforth 10/9/60
Edge Hill 9/9/61

## MILEAGES
| Year | Mileage |
|---|---|
| 1932 | 19,541 |
| 1933 | 72,849 |
| 1934 | 71,494 |
| 1935 | 68,912 |
| 1936 | 74,066 |
| 1937 | 73,993 |
| 1938 | 75,252 |
| 1939 | 61,437 |
| 1940 | 61,660 |
| 1941 | 37,084 |
| 1942 | 63,682 |
| 1943 | 42,428 |
| 1944 | 50,237 |
| 1945 | 42,700 |
| 1946 | 44,936 |
| 1947 | 33,888 |
| 1948 | 42,704 |
| 1949 | 37,697 |
| 1950 | 43,093 |
| 1951 | 41,989 |
| 1952 | 39,988 |
| 1953 | 42,014 |
| 1954 | 45,384 |
| 1955 | 41,471 |
| 1956 | 45,577 |
| 1957 | 38,833 |
| 1958 | 41,721 |
| 1959 | 45,294 |
| 1960 | 30,978 |
| 1961 | 31,191 |

**Mileage at 31/12/50 1,017,653 Lifetime mileage 1,462,093**
**Withdrawn week ending 15/9/62 from Edge Hill**
**Stored 15/11/61-withdrawal**
**Scrapped Crewe Works 10/62**

## TENDERS
| No | Fitted |
|---|---|
| 4485 | 19/9/32 |
| 4500 | 5/11/41 |
| 3927 | 5/10/50 |
| 4236 | 3/12/53 |
| 3190 | 5/11/54 |
| 3907 | 4/6/57 |
| 4490 | 5/2/59 |

*Below.* 45513, now with AWS and a Carnforth engine, passes Wortley Junction box, Leeds, with the down 1.54pm Leeds-Carnforth train, 7 June 1961. Photograph Gavin Morrison.

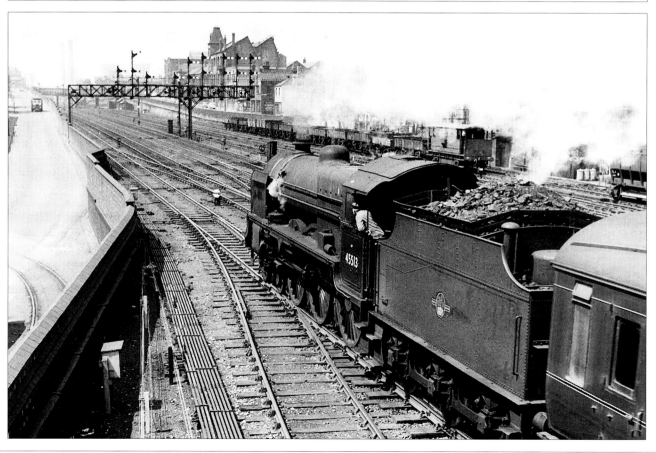

5514 in the 1930s at Camden with its name, HOLYHEAD, missing or blanked off. The RCTS *LMS Locomotive Names* reveals that it had the name 'briefly' in late 1938 so this photograph was presumably taken around that time. Photograph W. Hermiston, The Transport Treasury.

# 45514  HOLYHEAD (named briefly in 1938, then in March 1947)

Built Crewe 21/9/32 Replacement for 5983 (LNWR CLAUGHTON No 201)
*Renumbered 5983 to 5512 2/8/34*
*5514 to 45514 week ending 22/5/48*
*Converted to 6P (later 7P) 26/3/47 (4th of 18)*

**TENDERS**

| No | Fitted |
|---|---|
| 4486 | 21/9/32 |
| 9761 | 15/3/47 |

**MILEAGES**

| | |
|---|---|
| 1932 | 19,803 |
| 1933 | 67,664 |
| 1934 | 62,305 |
| 1935 | 63,412 |
| 1936 | 54,255 |
| 1937 | 49,434 |
| 1938 | 42,327 |
| 1939 | 47,269 |
| 1940 | 44,171 |
| 1941 | 50,253 |
| 1942 | 56,177 |
| 1943 | 41,957 |
| 1944 | 30,894 |
| 1945 | 42,314 |
| 1946 | 36,950 |
| 1947 | 48,072 |
| 1948 | 44,037 |
| 1949 | 50,436 |
| 1950 | 53,208 |
| 1951 | 74,124 |
| 1952 | 61,207 |
| 1953 | 60,169 |
| 1954 | 70,780 |
| 1955 | 55,533 |
| 1956 | 57,672 |
| 1957 | 58,061 |
| 1958 | 59,386 |
| 1959 | 57,066 |
| 1960 | 48,043 |
| 1961 | 467 |

**Mileage at 31/12/50 904,938**
**Lifetime mileage 1,507,446**
**Withdrawn week ending 27/5/61**
**after 'paper transfer' to Derby -**
**FIRST REBUILD TO BE**
**WITHDRAWN FROM**
**SERVICE**
**Scrapped Crewe Works 6/61**

**BOILERS**

| Fitted | Number | Received From | When Removed Passed To |
|---|---|---|---|
| 21/9/32 | | | 5948 |
| 24/10/34 | | 5908 | STOCK |
| 18/2/36 | | 5547 | 5516 |
| 3/5/37 | | 5534 | |
| 21/11/39 | 6005 | 5521 | 5542 |
| 18/6/41 | 6003 | 5540 | 5507 |
| 26/6/43 | 5357 | 5502 | 5501 |
| | | | |
| 26/3/47 | 12540 | NEW | 45531 |
| 30/12/50 | 13593 | NEW | 46137 |
| 8/3/55 | 12528 | 46127 | 45523 |
| 23/3/57 | 12660 | 46141 | |

**SHEDS**

Leeds 21/9/32
Camden 16/2/35
Shrewsbury 23/3/35
Aston 20/4/35
Preston 11/3/39
Carlisle Upperby 29/7/39
Longsight 31/5/41
Crewe North 18/7/42
Edge Hill 13/5/44
Longsight (Loan) 24/8/46
Edge Hill 21/9/46

Holyhead 17/5/47
Crewe North 21/6/47
Bushbury 19/7/47
Holyhead 7/8/48
Bushbury 2/10/48
Carlisle Upperby 28/5/49
Bushbury 1/10/49
Camden 10/6/50
Millhouses 2/60
Derby 27/5/61

**REPAIRS**

4/2/33-29/3/33**LO** (46)
4/1/34-25/1/34**LS** (19)
12/10/34-14/11/34**HG** (29)
4/2/36-26/2/36**HS** (20)
26/4/37-19/5/37**HG** (21)
23/8/38-22/9/38**HS** (27)
21/11/39-14/12/39**HG** (21)
22/3/41-5/4/41**LS** (13)
4/6/41-18/6/41**HO** (13)
24/2/42-10/3/42**LS** (13)
22/5/43-26/6/43**HG** (31)
23/9/43-7/10/43**LO** (13)
13/4/44-10/5/44**LO** (24)
2/6/44-28/6/44**TRO** (23)
31/3/45-2/5/45**HS** (28)

22/12/46-26/3/47**HG** (80)
19/4/48-22/5/48**HS** (30)
10/8/49-23/9/49**LI** (39)
28/9/49-4/10/49**NC (Rect)** (6)
26/4/50-3/5/50**LC** (6)
28/10/50-30/12/50**HG** (53) SMOKE
DEFLECTORS FITTED
2/1/51-20/1/51**NC(Rect)** (16)
1/1/52-30/1/52**LI** (25)
19/1/53-14/2/53**LI** (23)
23/6/53-6/8/53**LC** (38)
24/8/53-27/8/53**NC(Rect)EO** (3)
17/2/54-12/3/54**LI** (20)
10/1/55-8/3/55**HG** (49)
10/3/55-14/3/55**NC(Rect)EO** (3)
9/3/56-12/4/56**LI** (28)
9/2/57-23/3/57**HG** (36)
3/3/58-2/4/58**LI** (26)
5/9/58-3/10/58**LC(EO)** (24)
24/9/59-7/11/59**HI** (38) AWS GEAR FITTED

5514 was converted to taper boiler form in 1947, finally getting the name HOLYHEAD for good. It is north of Watford Tunnel on 30 August 1947 (unusually carrying a reporting number) and is in the post-war LMS black. As usual the photographer has recorded all the detail; the time was 9.45am and the train an up early morning express from Wolverhampton, probably checked and running at about 25mph – hence the blowing off. Photograph E.D. Bruton.

A Patriot in Scotland. They did go north of Carlisle, of course, though not very often – or not very often in daylight at weekends, for in a collection of several hundred photographs, only a handful are 'north of the border'. 45514 in BR green with deflectors is at Dalry Road shed, Edinburgh; Willie Hermiston, who along with John Robertson must have spent more time on Edinburgh and Glasgow sheds than some of the staff, was certainly impressed, because he photographed HOLYHEAD twice – see the introductory notes p11. Photograph W. Hermiston, The Transport Treasury.

# 45515 CAERNARVON (from 15/1/39)

**Built Crewe 27/9/32 Replacement for 5992 (LNWR CLAUGHTON No 2090)**
*Renumbered 5992 to 5515 21/8/34*
*5515 to 45515 week ending 24/4/48*

### TENDERS

| No | Fitted |
|---|---|
| 4487 | 27/9/32 |
| 4505 | 29/7/53 |
| 4509 | 4/1/56 |
| 4573 | 10/1/57 (HIGH STRAIGHT SIDED) |
| 3898 | 9/2/57 |
| 4570 | 17/8/57 (HIGH STRAIGHT SIDED) |
| 4487 | 15/3/58 |
| 4493 | 3/4/59 |
| 4489 | 25/10/60 |
| 3927 | 19/11/60 |

### MILEAGES

| Year | Mileage |
|---|---|
| 1932 | 21,248 |
| 1933 | 82,992 |
| 1934 | 62,498 |
| 1935 | 57,361 |
| 1936 | 58,644 |
| 1937 | 51,234 |
| 1938 | 43,395 |
| 1939 | 57,632 |
| 1940 | 58,231 |
| 1941 | 53,528 |
| 1942 | 42,996 |
| 1943 | 39,246 |
| 1944 | 39,678 |
| 1945 | 36,519 |
| 1946 | 41,591 |
| 1947 | 38,966 |
| 1948 | 46,011 |
| 1949 | 38,821 |
| 1950 | 47,923 |
| 1951 | 41,547 |
| 1952 | 35,138 |
| 1953 | 42,431 |
| 1954 | 41,128 |
| 1955 | 43,786 |
| 1956 | 44,630 |
| 1957 | 40,777 |
| 1958 | 37,418 |
| 1959 | 38,968 |
| 1960 | 33,882 |
| 1961 | 31,451 |

**Mileage at 31/12/50 918,514 Approx**
**Lifetime Mileage 1,375,000**
**Withdrawn week ending 9/6/62 from Newton Heath**
**Stored 26/3/62 - Withdrawal (at Bolton MPD 3/6/62)**
**Scrapped Crewe Works 8/62**

### BOILERS

| Fitted | Number | Received From | When Removed Passed To |
|---|---|---|---|
| 27/9/32 | | 5524 | |
| 2/8/34 | | 5521 | STOCK |
| 18/9/36 | | 5526 | |
| 24/1/39 | 5366 | 5910 | |
| 9/5/41 | 5352 | 5504 | |
| 18/1/44 | 5353 | 5546 | 45506 |
| 22/4/48 | 6010 | 5528 | 45533 |
| 15/5/51 | 5358 | 5539 | 45542 |
| 20/10/54 | 6008 | 45504 | 45504 |
| 15/3/58 | 6031 | 45543 | |
| 26/1/61 | 6010 | 45549 | WDL |

### SHEDS

Leeds 27/9/32
Carlisle Upperby 30/10/33
Leeds 3/11/34
Camden 16/2/35
Shrewsbury 23/3/35
Aston 20/4/35
Preston 11/3/39
Longsight 2/12/39
Aston 4/4/42
Preston 23/5/42
Crewe North 5/2/44
Bushbury 13/10/45
Carlisle Upperby 9/3/46
Preston 16/11/46
Edge Hill 19/11/49
Newton Heath (Loan) 2/4/60
Newton Heath 28/5/60

### REPAIRS

22/1/34-14/2/34**LS** (21)
18/7/34-21/8/34**HG** (30)
26/9/35-30/9/35**LO** (4)
22/11/35-11/12/35**HS** (17)
9/9/36-5/10/36**HG** (23)
25/8/37-13/9/37**HS** (17)
14/12/38-24/1/39**HG** (36)
6/4/40-24/4/40**LS** (16)
8/11/40-22/11/40**LO** (13)
17/4/41-9/5/41**HG** (20)
9/6/41-21/6/41**LO** (12)
21/12/42-14/2/43**LS** (21)
30/12/43-18/1/44**HG** (17)
10/9/45-6/10/45**HS** (24)
1/10/46-19/10/46**HS** (17)
11/3/48-22/4/48**HG** (36)
24/8/49-15/9/49**LI** (20)
6/4/51-15/5/51**HG** (33)
27/12/52-19/1/53**HI** (19)
25/7/53-4/9/53**HC** (35)
8/9/53-10/9/53**NC(Rect)EO** (2)
9/9/54-20/10/54**HG** (35)
1/11/54-4/11/54**NC(Rect)EO** (3)
8/12/55-4/1/56**LI** (21)
9/1/57-9/2/57**LC** (27)
11/1/58-15/3/58**HG** (54)
28/3/59-3/4/59**NC(EO)** (5)
21/9/59-17/10/59**HI** (23) AWS GEAR FITTED
10/11/60-26/1/61**HG** (64)

45515 CAERNARVON; it wasn't a 'resort', the RCTS account of names and their origins simply saying 'a town served by the company' and we can only be grateful that that particular theme was not extended to any dramatic degree...
It would be in LMS black and does look as pretty as a picture, at Oxenholme on 26 April 1949. Photograph H.C. Casserley.

45515 CAERNARVON, headed by 2-6-4T 42538 at Birmingham New Street on 28 November 1957, waiting to leave Platform 6 with the 2.0pm to Liverpool Lime Street and Manchester London Road. Note high sided tender 4570, attached for several months at this time. Photograph Michael Mensing.

45515 at New Street again, arriving with the stock for the 1.55pm to Liverpool and Manchester at Platform 6, 2 May 1959. The other engine on this occasion is Black Five 45390; note tender change. Photograph Michael Mensing.

# 45516 THE BEDFORDSHIRE AND HERTFORDSHIRE REGIMENT (from 31/7/38)

**Built Crewe 10/10/32 Replacement for 5982 (LNWR CLAUGHTON No.103)**
*Renumbered 5982 to 5516 28/5/34*
*5516 to 45516 week ending 12/2/49*

**MILEAGES**

| | |
|---|---|
| 1932 | 14,435 |
| 1933 | 51,994 |
| 1934 | 57,681 |
| 1935 | 52,080 |
| 1936 | 73,888 |
| 1937 | 68,001 |
| 1938 | 60,820 |
| 1939 | 56,044 |
| 1940 | 57,412 |
| 1941 | 60,568 |
| 1942 | 45,929 |
| 1943 | 40,790 |
| 1944 | 35,643 |
| 1945 | 42,391 |
| 1946 | 33,171 |
| 1947 | 35,097 |
| 1948 | 46,149 |
| 1949 | 38,162 |
| 1950 | 36,129 |
| 1951 | 43,473 |
| 1952 | 43,076 |
| 1953 | 41,182 |
| 1954 | 44,329 |
| 1955 | 35,358 |
| 1956 | 41,887 |
| 1957 | 44,640 |
| 1958 | 40,066 |
| 1959 | 38,822 |
| 1960 | 37,884 |
| 1961 | 13,443 |

**Mileage at 31/12/50 906,484 Lifetime Mileage 1,330,644**
**Withdrawn week ending 22/7/61 from Warrington**
**Scrapped Crewe Works 9/61**

**BOILERS**

| Fitted | Number | Received From | When Removed Passed To |
|---|---|---|---|
| 10/10/32 | | | 5974 |
| 6/10/33 | | 5908 | STOCK |
| 9/2/35 | | 5953 | 5546 |
| 31/5/37 | 6174 | 5514 | 5501 |
| 23/8/39 | 6173 | 5508 | 5506 |
| 1/1/42 | 6175 | 6023 | 5542 |
| 28/2/46 | 5997 | 5525 | 45539 |
| 22/8/50 | 5995 | 45510 | 45505 |
| 30/7/55 | 6173 | 45542 | 45551 |
| 22/2/58 | 5369 | 45539 | WDL |

**SHEDS**

Kentish Town 10/10/32
Patricroft 20/4/35
Camden 4/1/36
Longsight 31/5/41
Preston 28/3/42
Crewe North 3/10/42
Preston 5/6/43
Carlisle Upperby 15/9/51
Preston 5/7/52
Crewe North 20/9/52
Edge Hill 29/1/55
Crewe North 7/9/57
Edge Hill 21/9/57
Warrington 6/2/60

**TENDERS**

| No | Fitted |
|---|---|
| 4488 | 10/10/32 |
| 3187 | 23/2/35 |
| 3929 | 7/2/52 |
| 4554 | 29/12/53 |
| 3933 | 10/12/57 |
| 4554 | 22/2/58 |

**REPAIRS**

16/8/33-16/10/33**HS** (57)
1/2/35-4/3/35**HG** (27)
6/11/35-28/11/35**HS** (19)
7/5/36-9/6/36**HS** (29)
24/5/37-18/6/37**HG** (23)
13/6/38-23/7/38**LS** (36)
24/7/39-23/8/39**HG** (27)
6/11/40-23/11/40**LS** (16)
11/12/41-1/1/42**HG** (18)
20/2/43-24/3/43**LS** (28)
22/5/44-8/6/44**LO** (16)
18/9/44-3/10/44**HS** (14)
3/1/46-28/2/46**HG** (49)
26/3/46-26/4/46**LO** (27)
2/12/47-1/1/48**LS** (26)
17/1/49-9/2/49**HI** (21)
15/6/50-22/8/50**HG** (58)
7/1/52-7/2/52**LI** (27)
27/11/53-29/12/53**HI** (25)
28/5/55-30/7/55**HG** (54)
13/8/56-17/9/56**HI** (30)
5/12/57-22/2/58**HG** (66)
5/9/59-17/10/59**LI** (36) AWS GEAR FITTED

45516 THE BEDFORDSHIRE AND HERTFORDSHIRE REGIMENT south of Tring with an up train on the afternoon of 3 October 1953. This is fairly late to retain the BRITISH RAILWAYS on the tender which would mean it was still in black. It now has the 6P over the number ; when renumbered in February 1949 it still had the 5XP below the number of course, and for a while it ran with BR number and LMS on the tender. Photograph E.D. Bruton.

45517, not named throughout its career, in its Bank Hall days with a down express on Shap. Photograph Geoff Goslin, The Gresley Society.

45517 seemed to turn up in Scotland more than the other Patriots put together (a conclusion based, it must be said on the highly unrepresentative basis of photographs, which wouldn't survive any statistical test). It went to a former Central Division shed, Bank Hall, in 1958 and its regular use on the Glasgow jobs saw it frequently north of Carlisle. Here it is at Glasgow Central, returning south on 27 March 1959 with a Manchester relief and about to cross the Clyde. Photograph W.A.C. Smith.

# 45517

**Built Crewe 6/2/33 Replacement for 5952 (LNWR CLAUGHTON No.171)**
*Renumbered 5952 to 5517 14/7/34*
*            5517 to 45517 week ending 17/9/49*

## BOILERS

| Fitted | Number | Received From | When Removed Passed To |
|---|---|---|---|
| 6/2/33 | | | 5525 |
| 8/10/34 | | 5524 | STOCK |
| 17/10/35 | | 5927 | STOCK |
| 17/2/37 | | 5927 | STOCK |
| 14/1/38 | 5485 | 5545 | 5513 |
| 7/2/39 | 6006 | 5526 | 5523 |
| 24/10/42 | 5995 | 5523 | 5510 |
| 23/5/46 | 6003 | 5507 | 45551 |
| 15/9/49 | 5481 | 5545 | |
| 24/11/52 | 5975 | 45513 | 45548 |
| 9/4/56 | 6033 | 45524 | 45537 |
| 18/3/58 | 6009 | 45547 | WDL |

## TENDERS

| No | Fitted |
|---|---|
| 4489 | 6/2/33 |
| 4493 | 25/10/60 |

## MILEAGES

| | |
|---|---|
| 1933 | 73,656 |
| 1934 | 67,526 |
| 1935 | 69,533 |
| 1936 | 59,756 |
| 1937 | 65,921 |
| 1938 | 58,481 |
| 1939 | 50,927 |
| 1940 | 30,123 |
| 1941 | 45,165 |
| 1942 | 53,737 |
| 1943 | 49,532 |
| 1944 | 39,204 |
| 1945 | 38,696 |
| 1946 | 36,790 |
| 1947 | 41,345 |
| 1948 | 42,046 |
| 1949 | 32,206 |
| 1950 | 40,929 |
| 1951 | 39,814 |
| 1952 | 23,102 |
| 1953 | 52,519 |
| 1954 | 27,472 |
| 1955 | 41,831 |
| 1956 | 41,990 |
| 1957 | 45,339 |
| 1958 | 38,870 |
| 1959 | 53,137 |
| 1960 | 36,155 |

**Mileage at 31/12/50 895,573**
**Withdrawn week ending 9/6/62 from**
**Bank Hall**
**Stored 9/4/62 - Withdrawal**
**Scrapped Crewe Works 7/62**

## SHEDS

Camden 6/2/33
Edge Hill 16/3/35
Camden 6/7/35
Longsight 13/7/35
Aston 30/11/35
Preston 18/7/36
Crewe North 25/2/39
Preston (Loan) 11/3/39
Preston 1/4/39
Carlisle Upperby 16/9/39
Aston 6/1/40
Rugby 20/1/40
Longsight 31/5/41
Aston 25/4/42
Crewe North 23/5/42
Edge Hill 13/5/44
Crewe North 14/2/48
Carlisle Upperby 5/6/48
Willesden 13/6/53
Bank Hall (Loan) 26/7/58
Bank Hall 8/11/58

## REPAIRS

28/9/34-23/10/34**HG** (22)
8/10/35-29/10/35**HS** (19)
11/2/37-5/3/37**HG** (20)
3/1/38-20/1/38**HS** (17)
26/12/38-7/2/39**HG** (38)
22/7/40-3/8/40**LS** (12)
16/7/41-31/7/41**HS** (14)
2/10/42-24/10/42**HG** (20)
18/9/43-13/10/43**LO** (22)
4/10/44-19/10/44**HS** (14)
7/5/46-23/5/46**HG** (15)
2/12/47-24/1/48**HS** (46)
5/8/49-15/9/49**HG** (36)
17/10/49-25/10/49**NC** (8)
12/3/51-12/4/51**HI** (26)
25/8/52-24/11/52**HG** (78)
26/7/54-24/8/54**HI** (25)
18/2/56-9/4/56**HG** (42)
22/12/57-18/3/58**HG** (71)
13/5/59-6/6/59**HI** (21) AWS GEAR FITTED
17/10/60-2/12/60**HI** (40)

45518 BRADSHAW, another Patriot which was briefly named in the 1930s and then 'renamed' with the same name after the Second World War. BRADSHAW at Crewe North has the remnants of the 1946 livery, so worn as to be near-invisible. Engine pickers will note the four-hole bracket from the vacuum pump still on the crosshead and the bolted rectangle on the smoke deflector above the steam pipes. This was presumably a removable access plate, and was not present in the first years. Photograph W. Hermiston, The Transport Treasury.

45519 LADY GODIVA in the deep cutting into the slope of Jeffrey's Mount under the main A6, having just cleared Dillicar Troughs south of Tebay, Monday 26 May 1952. The train is the up Class H through freight from Upperby Yard to Winwick Quay, serving the Warrington/Manchester Ship Canal districts. Engine very dapper in BR green. Photograph E.D. Bruton.

LADY GODIVA, now with the second BR emblem, leaving Derby on 25 May 1959 with the northbound Devonian. The general plan was to apply the BR emblem (first or second one) in the small version on Fowler tenders. On Stanier tenders the larger version was used. The Lady was allocated to Bristol Barrow Road, along with 45504 and 45506. Photograph R.C. Riley, The Transport Treasury.

# 45518 BRADSHAW (briefly from 5/39 and again in early 1947)

**Built Crewe 20/2/33 Replacement for 6006 (LNWR CLAUGHTON No.68)**
*Renumbered 6006 to 5518 22/5/34*
*5518 to 45518 week ending 3/7/48*

## MILEAGES

| Year | Mileage |
|---|---|
| 1933 | 71,758 |
| 1934 | 55,819 |
| 1935 | 67,515 |
| 1936 | 75,287 |
| 1937 | 73,514 |
| 1938 | 75,200 |
| 1939 | 59,222 |
| 1940 | 56,677 |
| 1941 | 62,540 |
| 1942 | 54,004 |
| 1943 | 41,466 |
| 1944 | 34,566 |
| 1945 | 29,156 |
| 1946 | 30,449 |
| 1947 | 34,896 |
| 1948 | 37,800 |
| 1949 | 31,280 |
| 1950 | 44,934 |
| 1951 | 42,030 |
| 1952 | 40,781 |
| 1953 | 42,400 |
| 1954 | 47,336 |
| 1955 | 37,362 |
| 1956 | 41,743 |
| 1957 | 36,979 |
| 1958 | 43,009 |
| 1959 | 34,462 |
| 1960 | 38,331 |
| 1961 | 14,754 to 8 August |

**Mileage at 31/12/50 936,083 Approx Lifetime Mileage 1,360,000**
**Withdrawn week ending 20/10/62 from Lancaster**
**Stored 16/11/61-27/1/62 and 4/6/62 - Withdrawal**
**Scrapped Horwich Works 2/63**

## REPAIRS

21/2/34-8/3/34**LS** (14)
19/4/34-22/5/34**LO** (29)
8/1/35-5/2/35**HG** (25)
26/3/36-9/4/36**LS** (13)
5/4/37-3/5/37**HG** (25)
28/5/38-27/6/38**HS** (26)
22/5/39-9/6/39**HS** (17)
21/2/40-26/3/40**HG** (29)
12/8/41-28/8/41**LS** (15)
12/6/42-4/7/42**HG** (20)
3/2/44-19/2/44**LS** (15)
20/10/45-24/11/45**HS** (31)
24/4/47-27/6/47**HG** (56)
24/5/48-1/7/48**LS** (34)
3/12/49-23/12/49**HI** (18)
19/12/50-9/2/51**HG** (44)
4/6/52-4/7/52**HI** (26)
25/8/52-23/9/52**HC(EO)** (25)
2/11/53-26/11/53**HI** (21)
9/4/55-10/5/55**HG** (26)
28/3/56-11/5/56**LI** (37)
14/9/57-26/10/57**HG** (36)
20/9/58-24/10/58**LC** (29)
1/9/59-13/10/59**LI** (36) AWS GEAR FITTED
8/8/61-19/9/61**HI** (36)

## TENDERS

| No | Fitted |
|---|---|
| 4490 | 20/2/33 |
| 3922 | 24/10/58 |
| 3913 | 13/10/59 |

## SHEDS

Camden 20/2/33
Longsight 7/10/39
Aston 28/3/42
Willesden 2/5/42
Crewe North 3/5/47
Carlisle Upperby 16/8/47
Preston 13/6/53
Edge Hill 19/9/53
Warrington 6/2/60
Aston 18/6/60
Edge Hill 9/9/61
Lancaster 10/2/62

## BOILERS

| Fitted | Number | Received From | When Removed Passed To |
|---|---|---|---|
| 20/2/33 | | | 5523 |
| 16/1/35 | | 5512 | STOCK |
| 19/4/37 | | 5508 | STOCK |
| 16/6/38 | 6008 | 5535 | 5538 |
| 26/3/40 | 5365 | 5543 | 5512 |
| 4/7/42 | 6172 | 5525 | 45537 |
| 27/6/47 | 6029 | 5510 | 45551 |
| 9/2/51 | 6030 | 5534 | 45544 |
| 10/5/55 | 6172 | 45510 | 45544 |
| 26/10/57 | 5995 | 45505 | WDL |

# 45519 LADY GODIVA

**Built Crewe 25/2/33 Replacement for 6008 (LNWR CLAUGHTON No.110 *LADY GODIVA*)**
*Renumbered 6008 to 5519 28/6/34*
*5519 to 45519 week ending 4/12/48*

## BOILERS

| Fitted | Number | Received From | When Removed Passed To |
|---|---|---|---|
| 25/2/33 | | | 5986 |
| 15/6/34 | | 5971 | 5512 |
| 7/10/35 | | 5541 | STOCK |
| 22/9/36 | | 5535 | STOCK |
| 4/1/38 | 5996 | 5512 | 5539 |
| 6/9/40 | 6001 | 5548 | 5540 |
| 10/3/43 | 6009 | 5547 | 45543 |
| 1/7/47 | 6170 | 5542 | 45506 |
| 14/9/51 | 6031 | 5503 | 45543 |
| 31/1/56 | 5999 | 45544 | 45508 |
| 15/7/58 | 6007 | 45506 | WDL |

## MILEAGES

| Year | Mileage |
|---|---|
| 1933 | 68,047 |
| 1934 | 74,394 |
| 1935 | 65,740 |
| 1936 | 66,373 |
| 1937 | 52,365 |
| 1938 | 62,831 |
| 1939 | 56,851 |
| 1940 | 44,283 |
| 1941 | 44,911 |
| 1942 | 46,169 |
| 1943 | 50,417 |
| 1944 | 33,046 |
| 1945 | 39,287 |
| 1946 | 40,582 |
| 1947 | 37,955 |
| 1948 | 46,748 |
| 1949 | 47,503 |
| 1950 | 41,547 |
| 1951 | 38,872 |
| 1952 | 43,177 |
| 1953 | 45,335 |
| 1954 | 38,309 |
| 1955 | 42,452 |
| 1956 | 44,111 |
| 1957 | 51,476 |
| 1958 | 40,454 |

**Presumably to 15/11/58 only. 1959 48,168 to 16 December**
**Mileage at 31/12/50 919,049 Lifetime Mileage 1,366,224**
**Withdrawn week ending 17/3/62 from Bristol**
**Scrapped Crewe Works 3/62**

## TENDERS

| No | Fitted |
|---|---|
| 4491 | 25/2/33 |

## REPAIRS

4/6/34-29/6/34**HG** (23)
23/1/35-25/2/35**HS** (29)
30/9/35-21/10/35**HG** (19)
7/9/36-1/10/36**HS** (22)
11/6/37-17/6/37**LO** (6)
28/12/37-18/1/38**HG** (19)
19/8/38-31/8/38**LO** (11)
20/2/39-20/3/39**HS** (25)
16/8/40-6/9/40**HG** (19)
15/9/42-3/10/42**LS** (17)
6/2/43-10/3/43**HO** (28)
25/7/44-11/8/44**LS** (16)
13/1/46-31/1/46**HS** (16)
15/5/47-1/7/47**HG** (41)
11/11/48-2/12/48**LS** (19)
14/2/50-3/3/50**LI** (15)
19/6/50-21/7/50**LC** (28)
14/7/51-14/9/51**HG** (53)
17/4/53-13/5/53**HI** (22)
17/8/54-16/9/54**HI** (26)
12/12/55-31/1/56**HG** (41)
28/11/56-17/1/57**HI** (41)
15/6/58-15/7/58**HG** (25)
16/12/59-12/3/60**LI** (73)

## SHEDS

Camden 25/2/33
Crewe North 17/6/33
Edge Hill 23/9/33
Crewe North 2/1/37
Preston 1/5/37
Carlisle Upperby 16/9/39
Crewe North 6/1/40
Rugby 11/1/41
Longsight 28/2/42
Aston 21/3/42
Willesden 2/5/42
Camden 8/6/46
Carlisle Upperby 11/1/47
Preston 25/10/47
Carlisle Upperby 3/2/51
Preston 24/3/51
Longsight 2/10/54
Carlisle Upperby 9/6/56
Longsight 23/6/56
Carlisle Upperby 25/8/56
Preston 20/10/56
Longsight 17/11/56
Crewe North 14/6/58
Carlisle Upperby 20/9/58
Bristol 15/11/58

# 45520 LLANDUDNO (from 1937)

**Built Derby 17/2/33 Replacement for 5954 (LNWR CLAUGHTON No.1085)**
*Renumbered 5954 to 5520 25/9/34*
*5520 to 45520 week ending 3/7/48*

**TENDERS**

| No | Fitted |
|----|--------|
| 4499 | 17/2/33 |
| 4474 | 14/10/52 |
| 4479 | 7/3/55 |
| 4505 | 23/1/56 |
| 4482 | 13/5/61 |

**MILEAGES**

| | |
|------|--------|
| 1933 | 73,690 |
| 1934 | 73,593 |
| 1935 | 57,065 |
| 1936 | 67,306 |
| 1937 | 69,785 |
| 1938 | 75,134 |
| 1939 | 50,418 |
| 1940 | 52,025 |
| 1941 | 37,544 |
| 1942 | 37,086 |
| 1943 | 31,734 |
| 1944 | 42,939 |
| 1945 | 40,290 |
| 1946 | 48,662 |
| 1947 | 44,723 |
| 1948 | 42,767 |
| 1949 | 34,012 |
| 1950 | 47,597 |
| 1951 | 39,944 |
| 1952 | 40,022 |
| 1953 | 46,995 |
| 1954 | 46,649 |
| 1955 | 41,117 |
| 1956 | 38,926 |
| 1957 | 45,689 |
| 1958 | 32,539 |
| 1959 | 37,612 |
| 1960 | 41,638 |
| 1961 | 22,075 |
| 1962 | - |

**Mileage at 31/12/50 926,370 Lifetime Mileage 1,359,576**
**Withdrawn week ending 19/5/62 from Edge Hill**
**Stored 16/11/61 - Withdrawal Scrapped Crewe Works 6/62**

**SHEDS**

Kentish Town 25/2/33
Edge Hill 6/4/35
Longsight 5/6/48
Preston 18/6/55
Longsight 17/9/55
Edge Hill 31/12/60

**BOILERS**

| Fitted | Number | Received From | When Removed Passed To |
|--------|--------|--------------|------------------------|
| 17/2/33 | | | STOCK |
| 21/3/35 | | 5520 | STOCK |
| 16/4/36 | | 5514 | 5551 |
| 22/3/37 | 5352 | 5526 | |
| 14/3/38 | 6032 | 5547 | 5946 |
| 6/10/39 | 5998 | 5536 | 5505 |
| 21/4/44 | 5985 | 5500 | |
| 27/4/49 | 6176 | 5536 | 45550 |
| 14/10/52 | 6000 | 45546 | 45520 |
| 1/3/57 | 6000 | 45520 | WDL |

**REPAIRS**

7/3/34-27/3/34**HS** (18)
20/2/35-9/4/35**HG** (42)
25/3/36-24/4/36**HS** (26)
6/3/37-10/4/37**HG** (30)
4/10/37-16/10/37**LO** (12)
7/3/38-28/3/38**HS** (19)
22/10/38-10/11/38**HS** (17)
4/5/39-18/5/39**LO** (13)
6/10/39-10/11/39**HG** (31)
20/3/41-5/4/41**LS** (15)
12/11/41-6/12/41**HS** (22)
2/1/43-2/2/43**LS** (27)
28/9/43-12/10/43**TRO** (13)
4/4/44-21/4/44**HG** (16)
31/1/45-16/2/45**LO** (15)
5/11/45-29/11/45**HS** (22)
19/5/47-14/6/47**LS** (24)
31/5/48-2/7/48**LO** (29)
2/2/49-27/4/49**HG** (72)
2/12/49-29/12/49**LC** (23)
12/11/50-2/12/50**HI** (17)
13/11/51-3/12/51**LC(EO)** (17)
8/12/51-10/1/52**NC(EO)** (26)
29/7/52-14/10/52**HG** (66)
19/12/53-15/1/54**LI** (21)
5/2/55-7/3/55**HI** (25)
23/1/56-23/1/56**LC(TO)** (1)
19/3/56-28/4/56**HC** (34)
10/12/56-1/3/57**HG** (68)
16/9/58-21/10/58**LI** (39)
30/9/59-13/10/59**NC(EO)** (11) AWS GEAR FITTED
25/11/59-22/1/60**HI** (48)

5520, later named LLANDUDNO, in original LMS red and more or less 'as built' with crosshead-driven vacuum pump but with cylinder drain pipes cut back. The suspension bridge in the background indicates the location is Crewe North.

45521 RHYL, the second engine to be converted (in October 1946, and still with the Stanier style top feed cover) with The Red Rose, the 12.30pm Euston-Liverpool, at Hatch End on 27 July 1951. Note Bakerloo Line train in the distance, in the days when they ran to Watford Junction.

# 45521 RHYL (from 1937)

Built Derby 4/3/33 Replacement for 5933 (LNWR CLAUGHTON No.162)
*Renumbered 5933 to 5521 26/7/34*
*5521 to 45521 week ending 14/8/48*
*Converted to 6P (later 7P) 31/10/46 (2nd of 18)*

## BOILERS

| Fitted | Number | Received From | When Removed Passed To |
|---|---|---|---|
| 4/3/33 | | | 5515 |
| 9/7/34 | | 5510 | STOCK |
| 13/11/35 | | 5548 | 5533 |
| 18/12/36 | | 5519 | STOCK |
| 24/2/38 | 6005 | 5530 | 5514 |
| 20/9/39 | 5981 | 5509 | 5546 |
| 22/7/43 | 5988 | 5523 | 5500 |
| 31/10/46 | 12537 | NEW | 46109 |
| 31/10/49 | 12675 | NEW | 45522 |
| 14/3/52 | 12657 | 45540 | 45529 |
| 25/1/55 | 12666 | 45528 | 45522 |
| 15/8/57 | 12675 | 45540 | |

## REPAIRS

19/6/34-26/7/34**HG** (33)
5/11/35-25/11/35**HS** (18)
8/2/36-6/3/36**LO** (24)
13/7/36-28/7/36**LS** (14)
10/12/36-5/1/37**HG** (22)
18/3/37-31/5/37**LO** (63)
21/2/38-4/3/38**HS** (11)
31/1/39-13/2/39**LS** (12)
20/9/39-10/10/39**HG** (18)
13/8/41-28/8/41**HS** (14)
26/9/41-22/10/41**TRO** (23)
24/6/43-22/7/43**HG** (25)
26/4/45-16/5/45**HS** (17)

12/7/46-31/10/46**HG** (96)
2/7/48-10/8/48**LS** (34)
15/9/49-31/10/49**HG** (40) SMOKE DEFLECTORS FITTED
17/10/50-11/11/50**HI** (22)
8/3/51-5/4/51**LC** (23)
1/2/52-14/3/52**HG** (36)
5/6/53-6/7/53**LI** (26)
20/3/54-12/4/54**LC EO** (19)
18/12/54-25/1/55**HG** (30)
24/2/56-27/3/56**HI** (27)
7/10/56-2/11/56**LC(EO)** (22)
25/6/57-15/8/57**GEN** (44)
6/11/58-3/12/58**LI** (23)
31/10/59-5/12/59**LI** (30) AWS GEAR FITTED
28/4/61-31/5/61**LI** (28) SPEEDOMETER FITTED

## TENDERS

| No | Fitted |
|---|---|
| 4500 | 24/2/33 |
| 4485 | 22/10/41 |
| 9779 | 31/10/46 |
| 9753 | 24/2/53 |

## SHEDS

Kentish Town 25/3/33
Edge Hill 16/2/35
Bushbury 11/9/37
Crewe North 11/3/39
Rugby 28/10/39
Crewe North 5/6/43

Longsight 5/4/47
Holyhead 17/5/47
Edge Hill 21/6/47
Springs Branch 16/9/61

## MILEAGES

| | |
|---|---|
| 1933 | 54,738 |
| 1934 | 52,935 |
| 1935 | 58,909 |
| 1936 | 69,928 |
| 1937 | 56,363 |
| 1938 | 54,202 |
| 1939 | 51,565 |
| 1940 | 34,949 |
| 1941 | 38,336 |
| 1942 | 45,838 |
| 1943 | 39,844 |
| 1944 | 49,036 |
| 1945 | 43,944 |
| 1946 | 35,256 |
| 1947 | 57,891 |
| 1948 | 61,004 |
| 1949 | 63,109 |
| 1950 | 66,046 |
| 1951 | 59,928 |
| 1952 | 69,128 |
| 1953 | 55,167 |
| 1954 | 57,008 |
| 1955 | 58,536 |
| 1956 | 57,142 |
| 1957 | 58,858 |
| 1958 | 56,036 |
| 1959 | 59,286 |
| 1960 | 61,387 |
| 1961 | 35,864 |
| 1962 | 23,888 |
| 1963 | 16,837 |

**Mileage at 31/12/50 933,893 Lifetime**
**Mileage 1,602,958**
**Withdrawn week ending 28/9/63**
**from Springs Branch**
**Scrapped Crewe Works 11/63**

5522 PRESTATYN in what should be the red livery of LMS days though it is lost under the grime. It is at Polmadie with a Crewe North shed plate; the time would be just after the end of the Second World War; PRESTATYN left for Preston at the end of 1948 and only returned to Crewe as a newly rebuilt taper boiler engine. Photograph J. Robertson, The Transport Treasury.

# 45522 PRESTATYN (from 22/3/39)

**Built Derby 3/3/33 Replacement for 5973 (LNWR CLAUGHTON No.1741)**
*Renumbered 5973 to 5522 24/5/34*
*5522 to 45522 week ending 12/2/49*
*Converted to 6P (later 7P) 7/2/49 (last of 18)*

### TENDERS

| No | Fitted |
|---|---|
| 4501 | 3/3/33 |
| 4492 | 8/3/45 |
| 9762 | 31/12/48 |

### MILEAGES

| | |
|---|---|
| 1933 | 62,038 |
| 1934 | 75,968 |
| 1935 | 56,064 |
| 1936 | 55,869 |
| 1937 | 60,880 |
| 1938 | 62,164 |
| 1939 | 59,475 |
| 1940 | 46,035 |
| 1941 | 43,928 |
| 1942 | 32,994 |
| 1943 | 46,900 |
| 1944 | 39,956 |
| 1945 | 51,479 |
| 1946 | 46,904 |
| 1947 | 40,515 |
| 1948 | 35,276 |
| 1949 | 58,250 |
| 1950 | 62,898 |
| 1951 | 63,159 |
| 1952 | 64,720 |
| 1953 | 62,546 |
| 1954 | 71,172 |
| 1955 | 59,401 |
| 1956 | 63,594 |
| 1957 | 49,663 |
| 1958 | 50,038 |
| 1959 | 59,748 |
| 1960 | 51,858 |

**Mileage at 31/12/50 937,593**
**Mileage at 31/12/60 1,533,492**
**Withdrawn week ending 19/9/64**
**from Longsight**
**Scrapped Central Wagon Co**
**Ince, Wigan 6/65**

### BOILERS

| Fitted | Number | Received From | When Removed Passed To |
|---|---|---|---|
| 3/3/33 | | | 5520 |
| 25/2/35 | | 5958 | STOCK |
| 18/11/36 | | 5533 | STOCK |
| 30/12/37 | 5479 | 5500 | 5546 |
| 31/12/38 | 5976 | 5545 | 5530 |
| 12/9/42 | 6031 | 5512 | 5503 |
| 27/7/45 | 5980 | 5545 | |
| | | | |
| 7/2/49 | 12666 | NEW | 45528 |
| 10/5/52 | 12675 | 45521 | 45540 |
| 29/1/55 | 12664 | 45535 | 46167 |
| 25/10/57 | 12666 | 45521 | |

### SHEDS

Kentish Town 25/3/33
Bushbury 16/2/35
Crewe North 11/3/39
Rugby 14/12/40
Crewe North 5/6/43
Bushbury (Loan) 6/10/45
Crewe North 5/1/46
Preston 27/11/48

Crewe North 12/2/49
Longsight 18/6/49
Bushbury 1/10/49
Camden 10/6/50
Kentish Town (Loan) 28/11/59
Kentish Town 2/1/60
Newton Heath 16/9/61
Longsight 22/6/63

### REPAIRS

3/5/34-29/5/34**HS** (23)
23/11/34-7/12/34**LO** (13)
9/2/35-20/3/35**HG** (34)
3/6/36-17/6/36**HS** (13)
12/11/36-3/12/36**HG** (19)
21/12/37-5/1/38**HS** (13)
29/11/38-31/12/38**HG** (29)
3/1/39-18/1/39**LO** (14)
24/8/40-9/9/40**LS** (14)
8/7/42-12/9/42**HG** (58)
14/4/44-29/4/44**LS** (14)
6/7/45-27/7/45**HG** (19)
9/9/47-10/10/47**LS** (28)

11/10/48-7/2/49**HG** (102)
12/6/50-30/6/50**LI** (16)
13/4/51-9/5/51**LC** (22)
20/3/52-10/5/52**HG** (43) SMOKE
DEFLECTORS FITTED
20/5/53-27/5/53**NC(EO)** (6)
15/10/53-14/11/53**LI** (26)
31/12/54-29/1/55**HG** (25)
21/7/56-16/8/56**HI** (22)
28/8/57-25/10/57**HG** (50)
15/11/58-13/12/58**LI** (24)
8/10/59-19/11/59**HI** (36) AWS GEAR FITTED
29/12/60-11/2/61**HI** (38) SPEEDOMETER
FITTED

# 45523 BANGOR (from 1938)

**Built Crewe 8/3/33 Replacement for 6026 (LNWR CLAUGHTON No.211)**
*Renumbered 6026 to 5523 7/5/34*
           *5523 to 45523 week ending 9/10/48*
*Converted to 6P (later 7P) 8/10/48 (14th of 18)*

**TENDERS**

| No | Fitted |
|---|---|
| 4492 | 8/3/33 |
| 4501 | 8/3/45 |
| | |
| 9755 | 8/10/48 |
| 9370 | 4/8/52 |
| 9756 | 27/11/56 |

**MILEAGES**

| | |
|---|---|
| 1933 | 60,025 |
| 1934 | 74,029 |
| 1935 | 55,871 |
| 1936 | 57,598 |
| 1937 | 65,763 |
| 1938 | 48,469 |
| 1939 | 56,223 |
| 1940 | 38,420 |
| 1941 | 39,198 |
| 1942 | 45,185 |
| 1943 | 48,735 |
| 1944 | 47,345 |
| 1945 | 49,352 |
| 1946 | 36,442 |
| 1947 | 46,124 |
| 1948 | 40,458 |
| 1949 | 59,052 |
| 1950 | 50,025 |
| 1951 | 49,715 |
| 1952 | 53,370 |
| 1953 | 53,704 |
| 1954 | 73,480 |
| 1955 | 52,485 |
| 1956 | 52,459 |
| 1957 | 58,779 |
| 1958 | 61,791 |
| 1959 | 50,550 |
| 1960 | 53,983 |

**Mileage at 31/12/50 918,314 Mileage at 31/12/60 1,478,630**
**Withdrawn week ending 25/1/64 from Willesden**
**Stored 9/9/62-10/12/62 and 2/10/63 - Withdrawal**
**Scrapped Crewe Works 3/64**

**SHEDS**
Camden 25/3/33
Bushbury 23/3/35
Crewe North 6/4/35
Bushbury 28/9/35
Crewe North 11/3/39
Edge Hill 27/7/46
Crewe North 17/5/41
Edge Hill 29/12/45
Carlisle Upperby 5/6/48

Crewe North 16/10/48
Camden 7/7/51
Willesden 21/1/61

**BOILERS**

| Fitted | Number | Received From | When Removed Passed To |
|---|---|---|---|
| 8/3/33 | | | 5505 |
| 14/2/35 | | 5518 | STOCK |
| 23/11/36 | | 5532 | STOCK |
| 17/9/37 | 5367 | 5511 | |
| 13/9/38 | 5978 | 5518 | 5504 |
| 4/1/41 | 5988 | 5527 | 5521 |
| 16/12/42 | 6006 | 5517 | |
| 8/6/45 | 5977 | 5548 | 45538 |
| | | | |
| 8/10/48 | 12671 | NEW | 46165 |
| 25/3/52 | 12672 | 45545 | 45531 |
| 25/3/54 | 13244 | 46113 | 45512 |
| 19/6/57 | 12528 | 45514 | |

**REPAIRS**
16/4/34-7/5/34**HS** (19)
5/2/35-4/3/35**HG** (24)
11/12/35-7/1/36**LS** (23)
8/10/36-7/12/36**HG** (52)
6/9/37-27/9/37**HS** (19)
15/8/38-13/9/38**HG** (26)
1/2/40-23/2/40**HS** (20)
25/11/40-4/1/41**HG** (35)
8/9/41-11/10/41**LO** (30)
19/11/42-16/12/42**HS** (24)
21/6/44-15/7/44**LS** (22)
26/2/45-29/3/45 **HG** (17)
21/5/45-8/6/45**HG** (17)
10/1/47-5/2/47**HS** (23)

16/6/48-8/10/48**HG** (99)
28/6/50-4/8/50**LI** (32)
27/4/51-18/5/51**NC** (18)
2/2/52-25/3/52**HG** (44) SMOKE DEFLECTORS FITTED
29/8/53-22/9/53**HI** (20)
24/2/54-25/3/54**HG** (25)
10/1/55-8/2/55**HI** (25)
24/4/55-17/5/55**LC(EO)** (19)
22/6/56-28/7/56**HI** (31)
18/5/57-19/6/57**HG** (27)
28/8/57-21/9/57**NC(EO)** (21)
19/8/58-12/9/58**LI** (21)
2/12/59-13/1/60**HI** (34) AWS GEAR FITTED
15/5/61-15/6/61**HI(EO)** (27) SPEEDOMETER FITTED

**PRESTATYN rebuilt, on the 12.25pm Glasgow-Lockerbie at Motherwell, 23 March 1963. Photograph J.L. Stevenson, courtesy Hamish Stevenson.**

# 45524 BLACKPOOL

**Built Crewe 14/3/33 Replacement for 5907 (LNWR CLAUGHTON No.1319 SIR FREDERICK HARRISON)**
*Renumbered 5907 to 5524 19/7/34*
*5524 to 45524 week ending 12/2/49*
*RENAMED BLACKPOOL – date believed to be 23/3/36*

### TENDERS

| No | Fitted |
|---|---|
| 4493 | 14/3/33 |
| 4509 | 17/8/54 |
| 4512 | 26/11/55 |

### MILEAGES

| | |
|---|---|
| 1933 | 55,102 |
| 1934 | 63,797 |
| 1935 | 63,638 |
| 1936 | 74,240 |
| 1937 | 60,151 |
| 1938 | 59,043 |
| 1939 | 48,886 |
| 1940 | 47,661 |
| 1941 | 54,957 |
| 1942 | 43,105 |
| 1943 | 38,821 |
| 1944 | 39,221 |
| 1945 | 40,162 |
| 1946 | 36,003 |
| 1947 | 38,157 |
| 1948 | 44,609 |
| 1949 | 36,497 |
| 1950 | 40,667 |
| 1951 | 34,882 |
| 1952 | 36,605 |
| 1953 | 41,219 |
| 1954 | 37,915 |
| 1955 | 40,623 |
| 1956 | 50,366 |
| 1957 | 36,339 |
| 1958 | 44,335 |
| 1959 | 39,474 |
| 1960 | 23,618 |

**Mileage at 31/12/50 884,717 Mileage at 31/12/60 1,270,093**
**Withdrawn week ending 15/9/62 from Edge Hill**
**Stored 11/11/61 - Withdrawal Scrapped Crewe Works 10/62**

### BOILERS

| Fitted | Number | Received From | When Removed Passed To |
|---|---|---|---|
| 14/3/33 | | | 5908 |
| 13/9/34 | | 5992 | STOCK |
| 21/1/36 | | 5544 | 5520 |
| 22/2/37 | | 5510 | STOCK |
| 23/6/38 | | 5521 | |
| 26/6/39 | 5363 | 5541 | |
| 30/6/42 | 5479 | 5541 | |
| 25/8/45 | 6032 | 5525 | 45548 |
| 8/2/49 | 5986 | 5531 | 45549 |
| 31/5/52 | 6033 | 45503 | 45517 |
| 26/11/55 | 6175 | 45505 | 45547 |
| 21/9/57 | 5978 | 45501 | WDL |

### SHEDS

Patricroft 14/3/33
Camden 4/1/36
Preston 10/4/37
Carlisle Upperby 3/2/51
Preston 24/3/51
Carlisle Upperby 15/9/51
Carlisle Kingmoor (Loan) 5/7/52
Crewe North 2/8/52
Carlisle Upperby 29/1/55
Warrington 10/9/60
Edge Hill 10/6/61

### REPAIRS

2/3/34-21/3/34**LS** (17)
4/9/34-28/9/34**HG** (22)
6/1/36-28/1/36**HS** (20)
15/2/37-9/3/37**HG** (20)
2/4/37-24/4/37**LO** (20)
3/6/38-1/7/38**HS** (25)
25/5/39-26/6/39**HG** (28)
13/2/40-9/3/40**LO** (23)
26/11/40-14/12/40**LS** (17)
4/6/42-30/6/42**HG** (23)
9/4/43-7/5/43**LO** (25)
29/5/44-13/6/44**LS** (14)
9/8/45-25/8/45**HG** (15)
14/6/47-29/7/47**LS** (39)
3/1/49-8/2/49**HG** (32)
15/7/50-5/8/50**LI** (18)
7/8/50-18/8/50**NC(Rect)** (10)
21/2/52-31/5/52**HG** (85)
10/12/53-8/1/54**HI** (23)
13/2/54-2/3/54**LC(EO)** (14)
16/3/54-19/3/54**NC(EO)(Rect)** (3)
28/7/54-17/8/54**HC** (17)
25/10/55-26/11/55**HG** (28)
16/8/57-21/9/57**HG** (31)
1/1/58-8/2/58**LC(EO)** (33)
22/4/59-1/6/59**LI** (34) AWS GEAR FITTED
2/2/60-30/4/60**LC(EO)** (75)
6/3/61-11/4/61**HI** (30)

A difficult time lapse photograph lends an ethereal look to 5523, as yet not named and with the rest of the engine fading into background, at Euston in 1935. The 3B plate indicates Bushbury and the Patriot has presumably come up to town on a two hour 'Brum'. Photograph The Transport Treasury.

45523, rebuilt but bereft of its BANGOR plates, at Willesden on 6 October 1963. After ten years at Camden, it had gone to Willesden in January 1961. It spent three years there but for much of that time was in store, in part at Devons Road, Bow, where a dump was established in the old shed yard. Photograph Frank Hornby, The Transport Treasury.

45524 BLACKPOOL at Shrewsbury, ex-works from Crewe and accordingly in beautiful condition, 13 June 1952. Alongside is 5022 WIGMORE CASTLE, newly arrived from Plymouth; 45524 was about to take the train on to Manchester. B.K.B. Green, Initial Photographics.

# 45525 COLWYN BAY

Built Derby 22/3/33 Replacement for 5916 (LNWR CLAUGHTON No.856E TOOTAL BROADHURST)
*Renumbered 5916 to 5525 24/7/34*
*5525 to 45525 week ending 21/8/48*
*Converted to 6P (later 7P) 20/8/48 (11th of 18)*
*RENAMED COLWYN BAY 1937*

## TENDERS

| No | Fitted |
|----|--------|
| 4503 | 22/3/33 |
| 9757 | 20/8/48 |

## REPAIRS

1/3/34-22/3/34**HS** (19)
28/7/34-22/8/34**LO** (22)
16/10/34-21/11/34**HS** (19)
21/2/35-8/3/35**LO** (14)
30/10/35-13/11/35**LS** (13)
4/7/36-29/736**HS** (22)
1/6/37-25/6/37**HG** (22)
25/4/38-12/5/38**HS** (16)
7/6/39-30/6/39**HG** (21)
25/4/41-19/5/41**HS** (21)
26/5/41-7/6/41**LO** (12)
4/2/42-12/3/42**HG** (32)
7/8/43-27/8/43**HS** (18)
24/8/44-13/9/44**HG** (18)
27/5/46-25/6/46**HS** (26)
20/8/46-6/9/46**LO** (16)
22/11/46-27/12/46**LO** (30)

7/5/48-20/8/48**HG** (91)
6/12/49-16/1/50**LI** (34)
28/1/50-9/2/50**NC(Rect)** (10)
22/11/50-14/12/50**LI** (19)
29/10/51-1/12/51**LI EO** (29)
26/12/52-5/2/53**HG** (34) SMOKE DEFLECTORS FITTED
25/7/53-21/8/53**LC(EO)** (23)
22/4/54-15/5/54**HI** (20)
9/7/55-6/8/55**HI** (24)
20/8/55-16/9/55**LC(EO)** (23)
23/3/56-25/4/56**HG** (27)
12/11/56-14/12/56**HC(EO)** (28)
30/7/57-29/8/57**HI** (26)
12/9/58-16/10/58**HG** (29)
5/2/59-18/3/59**LC(EO)** (35) (AT RUGBY WORKS)
28/9/59-9/10/59**NC(EO)** (10) AWS GEAR FITTED
8/12/59-22/1/60**LI** (37)
10/10/60-12/11/60**HI** (29) SPEEDOMETER FITTED
10/8/61-22/9/61**LC(EO)** (37)

## BOILERS

| Fitted | Number | Received From | When Removed Passed To |
|--------|--------|---------------|------------------------|
| 22/3/33 | | | 5953 |
| 31/10/34 | | 5517 | STOCK |
| 20/7/36 | | 5545 | |
| 8/6/37 | 5365 | 5543 | 5507 |
| 14/5/38 | 6000 | 5542 | 5545 |
| 30/6/39 | 5997 | 5531 | 5516 |
| 12/3/42 | 6032 | 5946 | 5524 |
| 13/9/44 | 5994 | 6004 | 5508 |
| 25/6/46 | 5981 | 5546 | |
| | | | |
| 20/8/48 | 12656 | NEW | 45736 |
| 5/2/53 | 11730 | 45526 | 46118 |
| 25/4/56 | 11732 | 45532 | 46162 |
| 16/10/58 | 12539 | 46135 | |

## SHEDS

Kentish Town 25/3/33
Bushbury 28/9/35
Preston 11/3/39
Carlisle Upperby 16/9/39
Preston 4/10/41
Edge Hill 3/10/42
Longsight 25/1/47
Willesden 21/6/47

Crewe North 21/8/48
Bushbury 2/10/48
Carlisle Upperby 28/5/49
Bushbury 1/10/49
Carlisle Upperby 10/6/50
Crewe North 30/9/50
Camden 7/7/51
Crewe North 15/9/51
Camden 5/7/52
Crewe North 20/9/52
Edge Hill (Loan) 4/10/52
Edge Hill 3/1/53
Willesden 14/1/61
Llandudno Jct 23/9/61

## MILEAGES

| Year | Mileage |
|------|---------|
| 1933 | 52,422 |
| 1934 | 65,283 |
| 1935 | 50,589 |
| 1936 | 67,222 |
| 1937 | 59,785 |
| 1938 | 60,212 |
| 1939 | 47,428 |
| 1940 | 46,032 |
| 1941 | 37,890 |
| 1942 | 44,926 |
| 1943 | 38,350 |
| 1944 | 38,378 |
| 1945 | 44,825 |
| 1946 | 31,492 |
| 1947 | 40,208 |
| 1948 | 32,239 |
| 1949 | 50,721 |
| 1950 | 46,788 |
| 1951 | 48,741 |
| 1952 | 55,511 |
| 1953 | 61,095 |
| 1954 | 59,094 |
| 1955 | 39,678 |
| 1956 | 49,634 |
| 1957 | 67,028 |
| 1958 | 63,154 |
| 1959 | 52,394 |
| 1960 | 48,310 |
| 1961 | 38,013 |
| 1962 | 28,460 |
| 18/5/63 | 4,051 |

**Mileage at 31/12/50 854,790**
**Lifetime Mileage 1,469,953**
**Withdrawn week ending 11/5/63 from Llandudno Junction**
**Stored 4/11/62 to 3/2/63**
**Scrapped Crewe Works 6/63**

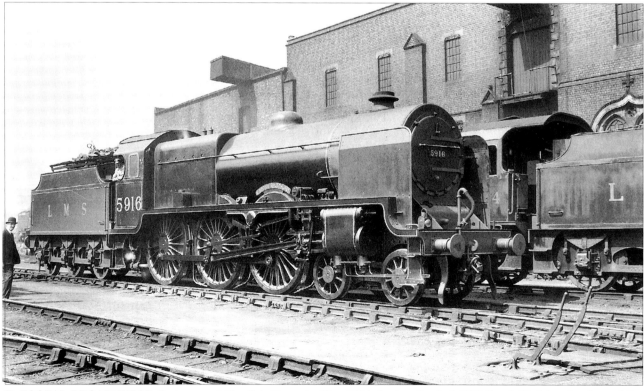

E. TOOTAL BROADHURST that was, at Kentish Town in May 1934 during the brief Midland Division heyday of the Patriots. It was renumbered 5525 a couple of months after this and renamed COLWYN BAY in 1937. Photograph W. Hermiston, The Transport Treasury.

45525 as COLWYN BAY, pre-deflectors, in 1948 recently converted to 2A taper boiler form; the livery would be the BR mixed traffic black, with Ivatt pattern top feed cover and slightly non-standard (and later replaced) smokebox numberplate. Photograph J. Paterson, The Transport Treasury.

# 45526 MORECAMBE AND HEYSHAM (from 6/10/37)

Built Derby 22/3/33 Replacement for 5963 (LNWR CLAUGHTON No 972)
*Renumbered 5963 to 5526 25/7/34*
*5526 to 45526 week ending 2/7/49*
*Converted to 6P (later 7P) 6/2/47 (3rd of 18)*

### TENDERS

| No | Fitted |
|---|---|
| 4502 | 22/3/33 |
| 9754 | 28/12/46 |

### REPAIRS
9/11/33-28/12/33**LS** (42)
13/4/35-23/5/35**HG** (34)
2/12/35-17/12/35**LS** (14)
17/4/36-30/4/36**HO** (12)
15/12/36-30/12/36**HS** (13)
23/9/37-1/10/37**HG** (8)
29/9/38-27/10/38**HS** (25)
24/7/39-24/8/39**LO** (28)
10/5/40-31/5/40**HG** (19)
12/2/42-13/2/42**TRO** (2)
22/4/42-20/5/42**LS** (25)
25/10/43-10/11/43**HG** (15)
15/5/45-15/6/45**LS** (28)
4/7/46-13/8/46**TRO** (35)

1/11/46-6/2/47**HG** (83)
11/1/48-7/2/48**LS** (24)
10/6/49-30/6/49**HI** (18)
14/4/50-20/4/50**LC** (5)
23/9/50-4/11/50**HG** (36) SMOKE DEFLECTORS FITTED
2/9/52-26/9/52**HG** (21)
27/1/54-12/2/54**HI** (14)
4/9/55-29/10/55**HG** (47)
31/1/57-23/2/57**LI** (20)
27/5/58-19/8/58**HG** (72)
24/9/59-13/11/59**HG** (43) AWS GEAR FITTED
19/1/61-17/2/61**LI** (25) SPEEDOMETER FITTED

### BOILERS

| Fitted | Number | Received From | When Removed Passed To |
|---|---|---|---|
| 22/3/33 | | | STOCK |
| 1/5/35 | | 5906 | 5515 |
| 23/4/36 | 5352 | 5903 | STOCK |
| 24/9/37 | 6006 | 5946 | 5517 |
| 27/10/38 | 5994 | 6017 | 6004 |
| 31/5/40 | 6010 | 5505 | 5528 |
| 10/11/43 | 5999 | 5517 | 45541 |
| | | | |
| 6/2/47 | 12529 | NEW | 45532 |
| 4/11/50 | 11730 | 46138 | 45525 |
| 26/9/52 | 12670 | | |
| 29/10/55 | 13238 | | |
| 19/8/58 | 12658 | | |
| 13/11/59 | 12668 | | |

### SHEDS
Leeds 25/3/33
Bushbury 16/2/35
Crewe North 11/3/39
Rugby 18/1/41
Edge Hill 5/6/43

Leeds (Loan) 28/6/47
Edge Hill 26/7/47
Bushbury 1/10/49
Carlisle Upperby 10/6/50

### MILEAGES
| | |
|---|---|
| 1933 | 44,257 |
| 1934 | 73,727 |
| 1935 | 51,510 |
| 1936 | 68,703 |
| 1937 | 62,947 |
| 1938 | 55,510 |
| 1939 | 54,162 |
| 1940 | 47,885 |
| 1941 | 40,409 |
| 1942 | 43,546 |
| 1943 | 30,023 |
| 1944 | 48,039 |
| 1945 | 47,396 |
| 1946 | 33,423 |
| 1947 | 64,317 |
| 1948 | 51,995 |
| 1949 | 60,076 |
| 1950 | 42,221 |
| 1951 | 63,864 |
| 1952 | 48,422 |
| 1953 | 57,627 |
| 1954 | 59,786 |
| 1955 | 44,359 |
| 1956 | 63,998 |
| 1957 | 57,156 |
| 1958 | 54,248 |
| 1959 | 62,366 |
| 1960 | 58,033 |

**Mileage at 31/12/50 920,146 Mileage at 31/12/60 1,490,005**
**Withdrawn week ending 24/10/64 from Carlisle Upperby**
**Scrapped T. W. Ward, Coatbridge 1/65**

45526 MORECAMBE AND HEYSHAM at Carlisle Upperby, 3 August 1953. Photograph Collection Hamish Stevenson.

# 45527 SOUTHPORT (from 1937)

**Built Derby 27/3/33 Replacement for 5944 (LNWR CLAUGHTON No.2411)**
*Renumbered 5944 to 5527 26/4/34*
*5527 to 45527 week ending 18/9/48*
*Converted to 6P (later 7P) 13/9/48 (12ᵗʰ of 18)*

## SHEDS
Camden 27/3/33
Edge Hill 16/12/33

Bushbury 4/3/61
Holyhead 6/5/61
Llandudno 10/6/61
Holyhead 9/9/61
Willesden 22/6/63
Carlisle Kingmoor 9/63
Carlisle Upperby 7/64
Carlisle Kingmoor 9/64

## REPAIRS
5/9/34-1/10/34**HG** (23)
11/10/35-7/11/35**HS** (24)
29/6/36-20/7/36**HO** (19)
20/12/36-18/1/37**HG** (24)
6/9/37-23/9/37**HS** (16)
9/6/38-21/6/38**HG** (38)
5/4/39-5/5/39**LO** (26)
8/10/39-3/11/39**LS** (23)
11/5/40-30/5/40**HG** (17)
23/7/41-6/8/41**LS** (13)
22/2/42-11/3/42**HO** (15)
16/1/43-13/2/43**LS** (25)
19/4/44-8/5/44**HG** (17)
30/4/45-26/5/45**HS** (23)
11/3/46-13/4/46**HO** (30)
14/1/47-31/1/47**LS** (16)

25/5/48-13/9/48**HG** (96)
25/4/49-18/5/49**LC** (21)
8/8/50-28/8/50**HI** (17)
18/10/51-23/11/51**HG** (31) SMOKE
DEFLECTORS FITTED
8/12/51-29/12/51**NC(EO)** (16)
21/2/53-31/3/53**HI** (32)
13/11/53-4/12/53**LI** (18)
21/7/54-21/8/54**HG** (27)
26/8/54-8/9/54**NC(Rect)EO** (11)
8/7/55-11/8/55**HI** (29)
3/4/56-9/5/56**HC** (31)
22/10/56-14/11/56**LC(EO)** (20)
17/5/57-29/6/57**HG** (37)
25/7/58-25/8/58**LI** (27)
13/2/59-7/3/59**LC(EO)** (19) AWS GEAR
FITTED
31/10/59-11/12/59**LI** (35)
8/8/60-10/9/60**HG** (29) SPEEDOMETER
FITTED

## TENDERS
| No | Fitted |
|----|--------|
| 4504 | 27/3/33 |
| | |
| 9753 | 13/9/48 |
| 9779 | 24/2/53 |
| 9765 | 22/6/59 |
| 9761 | 30/3/62 |

## BOILERS
| Fitted | Number | Received From | When Removed Passed To |
|--------|--------|---------------|------------------------|
| 27/3/33 | | | 5517 |
| 14/9/34 | | 5957 | SCRAP |
| 4/1/37 | | 6017 | |
| 2/6/38 | 5988 | 5510 | 5523 |
| 30/5/40 | 6178 | 5534 | 5541 |
| 11/3/42 | 6030 | 5532 | 5534 |
| 8/5/44 | 5483 | 5508 | 45500 |
| | | | |
| 13/9/48 | 12664 | NEW | 45535 |
| 23/11/51 | 12661 | 45531 | 46115 |
| 21/8/54 | 12028 | 46138 | 46158 |
| 29/6/57 | 13242 | 46113 | 45512 |
| 10/9/60 | 12203 | 46143 | |

## MILEAGES
| | |
|------|---------|
| 1933 | 46,456 |
| 1934 | 65,384 |
| 1935 | 52,801 |
| 1936 | 56,571 |
| 1937 | 72,692 |
| 1938 | 71,650 |
| 1939 | 52,477 |
| 1940 | 50,894 |
| 1941 | 42,162 |
| 1942 | 44,796 |
| 1943 | 41,863 |
| 1944 | 40,934 |
| 1945 | 38,123 |
| 1946 | 55,154 |
| 1947 | 41,242 |
| 1948 | 38,878 |
| 1949 | 67,206 |
| 1950 | 62,397 |
| 1951 | 57,041 |
| 1952 | 75,499 |
| 1953 | 55,671 |
| 1954 | 57,513 |
| 1955 | 63,794 |
| 1956 | 52,858 |
| 1957 | 64,964 |
| 1958 | 50,357 |
| 1959 | 50,958 |
| 1960 | 54,110 |

**Mileage at 31/12/50 941,680 Mileage at
31/12/60 1,524,445**
**Withdrawn week ending 5/12/64 from
Carlisle Kingmoor**
**Stored 6/1/63-16/6/63**
**Scrapped West of Scotland
Shipbreaking Co. Troon 2/65**

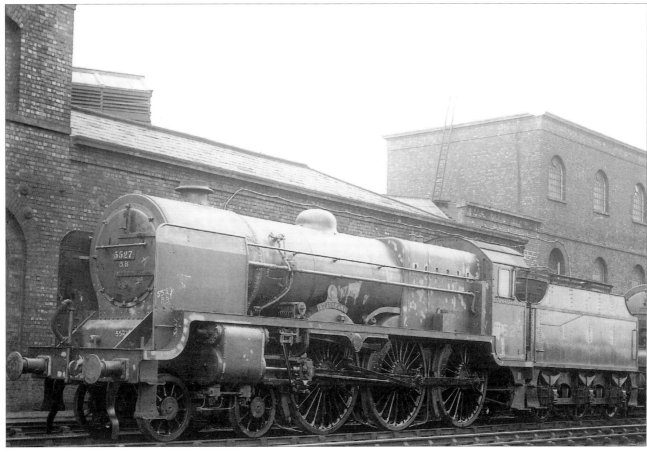

5527 SOUTHPORT, makes for an odd sight at Crewe Works on 12 June 1938. Various parts bear the painted '5527' to ensure they went back on the right engine, which is presumably awaiting entry to the Paint Shop.

45527 SOUTHPORT in the BR black, a fine sight at the dawn of BR, at Polmadie on 26 March 1950. Photograph Collection Hamish Stevenson.

# 45528 R.E.M.E. (from 2/10/59)

**Built Derby 4/4/33 Replacement for 5996 (LNWR CLAUGHTON No.10)**
*Renumbered 5996 to 5528 14/7/34*
*5528 to 45528 week ending 12/3/49*
*Converted to 6P (later 7P) 23/8/47 (6th of 18)*

### REPAIRS
6/12/34-21/12/34**HS** (14)
27/1/36-7/3/36**HG** (36)
9/10/37-4/11/37**HS** (23)
28/10/38-24/11/38**LS** (24)
31/7/39-19/9/39**LS** (44)
1/8/40-2/12/40**HG** (106)
17/2/41-8/3/41**LO** (18)
21/3/41-4/4/41**LO** (13)
8/10/41-30/10/41**LO** (20)
15/11/41-28/11/41**LO** (12)
5/12/42-14/1/43**LS** (34)
1/2/43-17/3/43**LO** (39)
23/2/44-11/3/44**HG** (16)
13/4/44-16/5/44**LO** (29)
8/11/44-22/11/44**HO** (13)
13/10/45-24/11/45**LS** (37)

23/4/47-21/8/47**HG** (104)
25/8/47-27/8/47**NC(Rect)** (3)
2/9/47-9/9/47**NC(Rect)** (7)
17/12/47-30/1/48**LO** (38)
7/2/49-9/3/49**LI** (27)
14/3/49-5/4/49**NC Rect** (20)
27/2/50-22/3/50**LI** (21)
4/4/51-26/4/51**LI** (19)
11/7/52-23/8/52**HG** (37) SMOKE
DEFLECTORS FITTED
28/9/52-4/10/52**LC(EO)** (5)
28/8/53-25/9/53**LI** (24)
30/9/54-5/11/54**HG** (31)
12/5/55-21/6/55**LC(EO)** (34)
25/8/55-29/9/55**LC** (30)
21/11/55-12/12/55**LC(TO)** (18)
16/4/56-22/5/56**LI** (31)
2/2/57-16/3/57**HG** (36)
27/8/58-24/9/58**HI** (24)
3/12/59-26/1/60**HG** (44) AWS GEAR FITTED
3/2/60-4/3/60**LC(EO)** (26)
24/7/61-26/8/61**LI** (29) SPEEDOMETER
FITTED

### BOILERS

| Fitted | Number | Received From | When Removed Passed To |
|---|---|---|---|
| 4/4/33 | | | |
| 6/12/34 | | | 5528 |
| 7/3/36 | | 5528 | |
| 11/3/44 | 6010 | 5526 | 45515 |
| | | | |
| 21/8/47 | 12541 | NEW | 45536 |
| 23/8/52 | 12666 | 45522 | 45521 |
| 5/11/54 | 12540 | 45531 | 46144 |
| 16/3/57 | 12663 | 45545 | 46118 |
| 26/1/60 | 12658 | 46140 | |

### SHEDS
Camden 4/4/33
Polmadie 11/5/35
Patricroft (Loan) 28/12/40
Patricroft 1/2/41
Edge Hill 27/9/46
Longsight 25/1/47

Bushbury 23/8/47
Crewe North 5/6/48
Longsight (Loan) 23/10/48
Crewe North 25/3/50
Camden 7/7/51
Crewe North 15/9/51
Camden 13/6/53
Crewe North 19/9/53
Camden 12/6/54
Crewe North 18/9/54
Longsight 19/2/55
Holyhead 26/3/55
Crewe North 7/5/55
Longsight 14/1/56
Crewe North 21/4/56
Holyhead 13/4/57
Crewe North 20/4/57
Willesden 14/1/61

### TENDERS

| No | Fitted |
|---|---|
| 4505 | 4/4/33 |
| 4484 | 7/7/34 |
| 4505 | 21/7/34 |
| 4469 | 30/1/44 |
| 4505 | 22/3/44 |
| | |
| 9782 | 21/8/47 |
| 9013 | 12/7/52 |
| 9782 | 5/11/52 |

### MILEAGES

| Year | Miles |
|---|---|
| 1933 | 46,365 |
| 1934 | 63,379 |
| 1935 | 82,210 |
| 1936 | 65,866 |
| 1937 | 47,463 |
| 1938 | 53,153 |
| 1939 | 54,770 |
| 1940 | 39,718 |
| 1941 | 29,051 |
| 1942 | 33,699 |
| 1943 | 37,394 |
| 1944 | 35,663 |
| 1945 | 40,880 |
| 1946 | 49,536 |
| 1947 | 30,927 |
| 1948 | 53,797 |
| 1949 | 62,083 |
| 1950 | 62,883 |
| 1951 | 55,174 |
| 1952 | 48,641 |
| 1953 | 65,276 |
| 1954 | 64,964 |
| 1955 | 49,698 |
| 1956 | 65,474 |
| 1957 | 57,314 |
| 1958 | 55,684 |
| 1959 | 54,409 |
| 1960 | 46,424 |

**Mileage at 31/12/50 888,837 Mileage at 31/12/60 1,451,895**
**Withdrawn week ending 19/1/63 from Willesden**
**Stored 9/9/62-10/12/62**
**Scrapped Crewe Works 3/63**

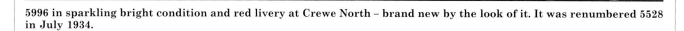

5996 in sparkling bright condition and red livery at Crewe North – brand new by the look of it. It was renumbered 5528 in July 1934.

45528 in final form with AWS gear and electrification flashes. The location is Willesden, its final home. This engine was curious in being named so late, getting its R.E.M.E. plates only in 1959. Photograph Paul Chancellor Collection.

5529 in the glorious LMS black at Camden shed, 31 August 1947. It did not get its name STEPHENSON until the following year, and the 'nameplate' is blank. An LMS stalwart labours on the never-ending ash deposits. Note the later replaced Stanier top feed cover. Photograph M.N. Bland, The Transport Treasury.

# 45529 STEPHENSON (from 24/7/48)

**Built Crewe 6/4/33 Replacement for 5926 (LNWR CLAUGHTON No.2204 SIR HERBERT WALKER, K.C.B.and apparently carried that name May-July 1933)**
*Renumbered 5926 to 5535 11/5/34*
*5535 to 45535 week ending 7/8/48*
*Converted to 6P (later 7P) 5/7/47 (5th of 18)*

### TENDERS

| No | Fitted |
|----|--------|
| 4495 | 6/4/33 |
| 3931 | 5/10/45 |
| 4495 | 2/5/46 |
| 9767 | 5/7/47 |

### REPAIRS

21/4/34-21/5/34**HS** (26)
21/5/35-18/6/35**HG** (25)
9/7/36-29/7/36**HS** (18)
28/5/37-23/6/37**HG** (23)
6/9/38-10/10/38**HS** (30)
26/9/39-27/10/39**HG** (28)
8/7/40-19/7/40**LS** (11)
12/10/40-20/12/40**HS** (60)
8/11/41-29/11/41**HS** (19)
27/10/42-28/11/42**HG** (29)
22/5/44-7/6/44**HS** (15)
14/9/45-5/10/45**LS** (19)
23/5/46-25/5/46**TO** (3)

21/4/47-5/7/47**HG** (66)
18/12/47-16/1/48**LO** (25)
8/7/48-7/8/48**NC** (27)
29/1/49-19/2/49**LI** (19)
20/5/50-12/6/50**HI** (19)
26/7/51-15/9/51**HG** (44) SMOKE DEFLECTORS FITTED
14/5/53-6/6/53**HI** (20)
8/3/55-23/4/55**HG** (39)
23/2/56-15/3/56**LC** (18)
24/4/57-21/5/57**LI** (23)
20/5/58-8/8/58**HG** (69)
21/9/59-3/10/59**NC(EO)** (11) AWS GEAR FITTED
4/2/60-18/3/60**LI** (37)
19/6/61-4/8/61**HI** (40) SPEEDOMETER FITTED

### SHEDS

Patricroft 6/4/33
Camden 4/1/36
Aston 25/9/37
Crewe North 11/3/39
Patricroft 6/6/42
Edge Hill 3/10/42

Bushbury 19/7/47
Camden 5/6/48
Bushbury 2/10/48
Crewe North 28/5/49
Camden 5/7/52
Crewe North 20/9/52
Camden 13/6/53
Crewe North 19/9/53
Camden 21/11/53
Crewe North 2/1/54
Camden 29/3/58
Crewe North 19/4/58
Willesden 14/1/61
Annesley 10/63

### BOILERS

| Fitted | Number | Received From | When Removed Passed To |
|--------|--------|---------------|------------------------|
| 6/4/33 | | | 5529 |
| 21/5/34 | | 5529 | STOCK |
| 29/5/35 | | 5534 | |
| 3/6/37 | 6029 | 5506 | 5539 |
| 10/10/38 | 5985 | 5507 | 5500 |
| 26/9/39 | 5989 | 5538 | |
| 20/12/40 | 6029 | 5539 | 5510 |
| 29/11/41 | 6004 | 5504 | 5504 |
| 28/11/42 | 6174 | 5501 | 5548 |
| 7/6/44 | 5984 | 5537 | 5511 |
| 5/7/47 | 12539 | NEW | |
| 15/9/51 | 13891 | NEW | 45736 |
| 23/4/55 | 12657 | 45521 | 46105 |
| 8/8/58 | 13593 | 46137 | |

### MILEAGES

| | |
|------|--------|
| 1933 | 47,118 |
| 1934 | 61,504 |
| 1935 | 62,174 |
| 1936 | 67,231 |
| 1937 | 67,479 |
| 1938 | 45,844 |
| 1939 | 42,568 |
| 1940 | 40,535 |
| 1941 | 52,848 |
| 1942 | 46,007 |
| 1943 | 45,505 |
| 1944 | 36,945 |
| 1945 | 38,403 |
| 1946 | 42,986 |
| 1947 | 41,419 |
| 1948 | 53,977 |
| 1949 | 55,712 |
| 1950 | 56,657 |
| 1951 | 51,161 |
| 1952 | 61,319 |
| 1953 | 57,183 |
| 1954 | 51,814 |
| 1955 | 51,895 |
| 1956 | 59,214 |
| 1957 | 50,417 |
| 1958 | 48,884 |
| 1959 | 55,352 |
| 1960 | 55,968 |
| 1961 | 34,050 |
| 1962 | 29,646 |
| 1963 | 31,541 |

**Mileage at 31/12/50 904,912 Final Mileage 1,543,356**
**Withdrawn week ending 22/2/64 from Annesley**
**Stored 14/10/62-10/12/62**
**Scrapped Crewe Works 3/64**

45529 STEPHENSON, a Patriot which ended up at Annesley, heading for Euston after availing itself of Bushey troughs, July 1953

# 45530 SIR FRANK REE (from 10/3/37)

**Built Crewe 3/4/33 Replacement for 6022 (LNWR CLAUGHTON No.205)**
*Renumbered 6022 to 5530 2/8/34*
*5530 to 45530 week ending 10/4/48*
*Converted to 6P (later 7P) 19/10/46 (first of 18)*

**REPAIRS**
11/7/34-2/8/34**HS** (20)
23/4/35-13/5/35**LS** (18)
18/11/35-17/12/35**HG** (26)
18/2/37-9/3/37**HS** (17)
10/1/38-11/2/38**HG** (29)
3/2/39-1/3/39**HS** (23)
28/10/39-18/12/39**HG** (44)
11/8/41-28/8/41**LS** (16)
27/2/42-1/4/42**LO** (29)
22/9/42-9/10/42**HG** (16)
28/5/43-17/6/43**LO** (18)
15/1/44-29/1/44**HS** (13)
14/2/44-25/2/44**LO** (11)
27/10/44-22/11/44**HS** (23)
24/5/45-21/6/45**LO** (25)

10/6/46-19/10/46**HG** (114)
24/1/48-18/3/48**LS** (22)
15/3/48-5/4/48**LO** (18)
22/1/49-17/2/49**LI** (23)
27/3/50-20/4/50**LI** (20)
14/10/50-11/11/50**HG** (24) SMOKE
DEFLECTORS FITTED
9/11/51-14/12/51**HI** (30)
27/12/51-19/1/52**LC** (20)
1/2/52-14/2/52**NC(Rect)** (11)
15/1/53-13/3/53**HG** (49)
13/4/53-2/5/53**NC(EO)** (17)
5/4/54-24/4/54**HI** (16)
5/3/55-11/5/55**HG** (56)
24/5/56-20/6/56**LI** (23)
1/11/56-24/11/56**HI** (20)
1/10/57-1/11/57**HG** (27)
1/12/58-6/1/59**LI** (29)
16/3/59-24/3/59**NC(EO)** (7) AWS GEAR
FITTED
26/2/60-1/4/60**LI** (30)
19/6/60-3/8/60**LC(EO)** (38)
19/5/62 SPEEDOMETER FITTED

**BOILERS**

| Fitted | Number | Received From | When Removed Passed To |
|--------|--------|---------------|------------------------|
| 3/4/33 | | | STOCK |
| 29/11/35 | | 5517 | |
| 31/1/38 | 5371 | 5511 | 5510 |
| 28/10/39 | 5480 | 5545 | 5501 |
| 9/10/42 | 5976 | 5522 | |
| 22/11/44 | 6007 | 5528 | 5538 |
| 19/10/46 | 12535 | NEW | 46147 |
| 11/11/50 | 12658 | 46162 | 46102 |
| 13/3/53 | 12197 | | |
| 11/5/55 | 12032 | | |
| 1/11/57 | 13243 | | |

**SHEDS**
Patricroft 3/4/33
Camden 4/1/36
Crewe North 20/2/37
Camden 10/4/37
Crewe North 10/2/40

Longsight 5/4/47
Leeds (loan) 17/4/48
Longsight 15/5/48
Northwich 25/4/59
Longsight 13/6/59
Camden 10/9/60
Willesden 10/6/61
Llandudno Jct 23/9/61
Willesden 7/7/62
Holyhead 6/64
Carlisle Kingmoor 1/65

**TENDERS**

| No | Fitted |
|----|--------|
| 4494 | 3/4/33 |
| 9772 | 19/10/46 |

**MILEAGES**

| | |
|------|--------|
| 1933 | 50,718 |
| 1934 | 64,415 |
| 1935 | 47,193 |
| 1936 | 80,477 |
| 1937 | 73,341 |
| 1938 | 74,278 |
| 1939 | 55,788 |
| 1940 | 50,825 |
| 1941 | 53,544 |
| 1942 | 42,391 |
| 1943 | 46,042 |
| 1944 | 51,577 |
| 1945 | 50,976 |
| 1946 | 31,764 |
| 1947 | 66,334 |
| 1948 | 60,609 |
| 1949 | 64,580 |
| 1950 | 60,694 |
| 1951 | 65,376 |
| 1952 | 66,524 |
| 1953 | 57,702 |
| 1954 | 63,239 |
| 1955 | 54,882 |
| 1956 | 57,319 |
| 1957 | 67,273 |
| 1958 | 62,981 |
| 1959 | 63,052 |
| 1960 | 47,229 |
| 1961 | 37,869 |
| 1962 | 18,438 |
| 1963 | 22,589 |

**Mileage at 31/12/50 1,025,546**
**Approximate Lifetime Mileage 1,740,000**
**Withdrawn week ending 1/1/66 from Carlisle Kingmoor Last rebuild to be withdrawn from service**
**Stored 14/10/62-10/12/62, 3/10/63-26/1/64 and 1/11/64-22/12/64**
**Scrapped Motherwell Machinery & Scrap Co., Wishaw 3/66**

45530 SIR FRANK REE at Willesden, its home for spells in the early 1960s, 27 July 1963. It was evidently highly prized at the London shed, for it was kept in perfect condition despite periods in store at Bow. On return from store the nameplates would be refixed and the engine was restored to such good condition that observers at Lostock Hall thought it had been specially repainted. Its condition, *The Railway Observer* declared, was such that that could rival an engine selected for the Royal Train! AWS and speedo, grab iron now above step. Photograph Peter Groom.

45531 SIR FREDERICK HARRISON leaving Platform 6 at New Street with the 3.55pm to Manchester London Road on 13 April 1957. Handrail on smoke deflector. Photograph Michael Mensing.

Fall from grace. SIR FREDERICK, AWS fitted and still with nameplates, in terrible condition and with the ghastly cab stripe, at its penultimate home, Upperby, on 30 August 1964. Someone, curiously, has rubbed off the thick grime at the lower front corner of the cab, uncovering some of the lining; whether this was to prove a point (yes, it *is* green) or it was rapidly abandoned as the sheer scale of the job became apparent must remain unknown. Photograph Paul Chancellor Collection.

# 45531 SIR FREDERICK HARRISON (from 1937)

**Built Crewe 7/4/33 Replacement for 6027 (LNWR CLAUGHTON No.517)**
*Renumbered 6027 to 5531 1/6/34*
            *5531 to 45531 week ending 22/5/48*
*Converted to 6P (later 7P) 13/12/47 (8th of 18)*

**TENDERS**

| No | Fitted |
|----|--------|
| 4496 | 7/4/33 |
| 9756 | 13/12/47 |
| 9370 | 27/11/56 |

**REPAIRS**

16/5/34-1/6/34**LS** (15)
31/12/34-8/2/35**HG** (35)
27/9/35-14/10/35**LS** (15)
21/10/36-28/11/36**HG** (34)
4/1/38-21/1/38**HS** (16)
1/2/39-2/3/39**HG** (26)
15/7/40-27/7/40**LS** (12)
16/9/41-1/10/41**HG** (14)
2/1/43-4/2/43**HS** (29)
1/11/43-26/11/43**HS** (23)
17/10/44-1/11/44**HG** (14)
7/5/45-19/5/45**TRO** (11)
14/4/46-4/5/46**LS** (17)

---

8/8/47-13/12/47**HG** (110)
5/5/48-20/5/48**NC** (14) THIS MAY HAVE BEEN A 'NO REPAIR' VISIT TO DERBY FOR REPAINT IN EXPERIMENTAL LIGHT GREEN LIVERY, AS WAS 45540
12/3/49-13/4/49**LI** (28)
22/3/50-29/3/50**LC** (6)
16/6/50-31/7/50**HI** (38)
1/6/51-28/7/51**HG** (49) SMOKE DEFLECTORS FITTED
12/1/53-17/2/53**HI** (31)
14/8/53-4/9/53**LC(EO)** (18)
28/5/54-18/6/54**HG** (18)
25/3/55-25/4/55**LI** (25)
5/6/56-6/7/56**HG** (27)
19/11/56-21/12/56**LC** (28)
15/11/57-12/12/57**HI** (23)
15/11/58-12/12/58**LI** (23)
21/5/59-13/6/59**NC(EO)** (20) AWS GEAR FITTED
18/8/59-17/9/59**LI** (26)
17/11/59-12/12/59**HC(EO)** (22)
14/7/60-20/8/60**LC(EO)** (32)
25/3/61-3/5/61**HI** (32) SPEEDOMETER FITTED

**BOILERS**

| Fitted | Number | Received From | When Removed Passed To |
|--------|--------|---------------|------------------------|
| 7/4/33 | | | 5970 |
| 9/1/35 | | 6013 | STOCK |
| 10/11/36 | | 5520 | |
| 2/3/39 | 5359 | 5511 | 5539 |
| 1/10/41 | 6171 | 5503 | 5503 |
| 1/11/44 | 5956 | 5948 | 45524 |
| | | | |
| 13/12/47 | 12661 | NEW | 45527 |
| 28/7/51 | 12540 | 45514 | 45528 |
| 18/6/54 | 12672 | 45523 | 46141 |
| 6/7/56 | 13895 | 46110 | 46151 |
| 12/12/59 | 12536 | 46142 | |

**SHEDS**

Patricroft 7/4/33
Bushbury 6/4/35
Camden 28/9/35
Willesden 20/11/37
Aston 11/6/38
Willesden 11/3/39
Camden 5/6/43
Bushbury 20/5/44
Crewe North 9/3/46
Longsight (Loan) 24/8/46
Crewe North 28/9/46

Bushbury 20/12/47
Camden 28/5/49
Bushbury 1/10/49
Edge Hill 10/6/50
Springs Branch 19/10/63
Carlisle Upperby 7/64
Carlisle Kingmoor 9/64

**MILEAGES**

| | |
|---|---|
| 1933 | 56,544 |
| 1934 | 74,298 |
| 1935 | 58,741 |
| 1936 | 69,420 |
| 1937 | 76,187 |
| 1938 | 50,218 |
| 1939 | 52,206 |
| 1940 | 41,447 |
| 1941 | 44,364 |
| 1942 | 52,412 |
| 1943 | 55,506 |
| 1944 | 53,286 |
| 1945 | 56,721 |
| 1946 | 45,433 |
| 1947 | 24,996 |
| 1948 | 56,801 |
| 1949 | 60,605 |
| 1950 | 51,346 |
| 1951 | 54,319 |
| 1952 | 62,351 |
| 1953 | 56,465 |
| 1954 | 60,012 |
| 1955 | 62,341 |
| 1956 | 53,179 |
| 1957 | 69,612 |
| 1958 | 60,442 |
| 1959 | 58,647 |
| 1960 | 51,689 |

**Mileage at 31/12/50 980,531**
**Mileage at 31/10/60 1,569,588**
**Withdrawn week ending 30/10/65 from Carlisle Kingmoor**
**Stored 6/10/62-2/2/63**
**Scrapped G H Campbell & Co., Airdrie 1/66**

**45532 ILLUSTRIOUS at Nottingham shed, an unusual and maybe unique case of a Patriot, having gone there originally, returning to the Midland Division. 14 April 1961. Photograph Peter Groom.**

# 45532 ILLUSTRIOUS

**Built Crewe 11/4/33 Replacement for 6011 (LNWR CLAUGHTON No.150 ILLUSTRIOUS)**
*Renumbered 6011 to 5532 14/8/34*
*5532 to 45532 week ending 3/7/48*
*Converted to 6P (later 7P) 3/7/48 (9th of 18)*

### TENDERS

| No | Fitted |
|----|--------|
| 4497 | 11/4/33 |
| 9760 | 3/7/48 |

### REPAIRS

7/7/34-14/8/34**HG** (33)
20/3/35-11/4/35**LS** (20)
28/3/36-14/4/36**HS** (14)
1/12/36-28/12/36**HG** (23)
5/10/37-2/11/37**HS** (25)
5/9/38-4/10/38**HG** (26)
5/9/39-3/10/39**HS** (25)
11/4/41-30/4/41**LS** (17)
13/1/42-31/1/42**HG** (17)
27/8/43-16/9/43**HS** (18)
5/1/45-3/2/45**HG** (26)
31/7/46-15/8/46**LS** (14)

23/3/48-3/7/48**HG** (88)
18/2/50-6/4/50**LI** (40)
14/7/51-18/8/51**HG** (30) SMOKE DEFLECTORS FITTED
10/9/52-6/10/52**LI** (22)
3/5/53-3/6/53**HG** (26)
10/8/53-11/9/53**HC(EO)** (28)
16/6/54-22/7/54**LI** (31)
14/10/55-1/12/55**HG** (41)
25/4/56-16/5/56**LC(EO)** (18)
5/3/57-5/4/57**LI** (27)
18/9/57-26/10/57**HI** (33)
20/3/58-16/4/58**NC(EO)** (22)
2/10/58-7/11/58**HG** (31)
23/9/59-6/11/59**LI** (38) AWS GEAR FITTED
11/11/60-5/1/61**HG** (45) SPEEDOMETER FITTED

### SHEDS

Leeds 11/4/33
Bushbury 16/2/35
Crewe North 11/3/39

Holyhead (Loan) 17/7/48
Bushbury 7/8/48
Camden 28/5/49
Holyhead (Loan) 15/7/50
Camden 12/8/50
Nottingham 21/11/59
Saltley 17/6/61
Derby 7/4/62
Carlisle Upperby 30/6/62

### BOILERS

| Fitted | Number | Received From | When Removed Passed To |
|--------|--------|---------------|------------------------|
| 11/4/33 | | | STOCK |
| 31/7/34 | | 5936 | STOCK |
| 2/4/36 | | 5524 | 5510 |
| 14/12/36 | | 6023 | |
| 4/10/38 | 5354 | 5551 | |
| 3/10/39 | 6030 | 5513 | 5527 |
| 31/1/42 | 5359 | 5531 | 5539 |
| 16/9/43 | 5978 | 5504 | 5537 |
| 3/2/45 | 6000 | 5505 | 45546 |
| 3/7/48 | 12667 | NEW | 46154 |
| 18/8/51 | 12529 | 45526 | 45526 |
| 3/6/53 | 11732 | 46150 | 45525 |
| 1/12/55 | 11726 | 46150 | 45735 |
| 7/11/58 | 13238 | 46123 | |
| 5/1/61 | 13241 | 46151 | |

### MILEAGES

| | |
|------|--------|
| 1933 | 63,200 |
| 1934 | 69,253 |
| 1935 | 58,043 |
| 1936 | 61,064 |
| 1937 | 65,771 |
| 1938 | 54,992 |
| 1939 | 51,512 |
| 1940 | 51,227 |
| 1941 | 48,374 |
| 1942 | 48,133 |
| 1943 | 45,476 |
| 1944 | 44,588 |
| 1945 | 49,132 |
| 1946 | 44,615 |
| 1947 | 43,185 |
| 1948 | 40,933 |
| 1949 | 58,670 |
| 1950 | 72,941 |
| 1951 | 60,410 |
| 1952 | 66,072 |
| 1953 | 63,940 |
| 1954 | 66,248 |
| 1955 | 57,835 |
| 1956 | 67,713 |
| 1957 | 52,913 |
| 1958 | 60,949 |
| 1959 | 63,560 |
| 1960 | 57,845 |

**Mileage at 31/12/50 971,109 Mileage at 31/12/60 1,588,594**
**Withdrawn week ending 1/2/64 from Carlisle Upperby**
**Stored 4/6/62-28/6/62**
**Scrapped G H Campbell & Co., Airdrie 12/64**

45533 LORD RATHMORE (the name came from a former LNWR Director and was carried by the preceding Claughton) was never converted to 2A form; on 5 July 1958 it is arriving at Platform 6 Birmingham New Street with the stock to form the 3.55pm to Manchester. Photograph Michael Mensing.

# 45533 LORD RATHMORE

**Built Derby 10/4/33 Replacement for 5905 (LNWR CLAUGHTON No.650 LORD RATHMORE)**
*Renumbered 5905 to 5533 18/9/34*
*5533 to 45533 week ending 5/2/49*

### TENDERS

| No | Fitted |
|----|--------|
| 4506 | 10/4/33 |
| 4488 | 15/3/61 |

### SHEDS
Kentish Town 10/4/33
Bushbury 28/9/35
Crewe North (Loan) 20/11/37
Bushbury 11/12/37
Crewe North 11/3/39
Patricroft 30/9/39
Springs Branch 16/3/40
Crewe North 8/6/40
Preston 22/6/40
Edge Hill 3/10/42
Willesden 23/10/42
Camden 5/6/43
Bushbury 20/5/44
Edge Hill 9/3/46
Carlisle Upperby 27/9/58
Rugby 21/11/59
Nuneaton 31/12/60
Edge Hill 16/9/61

### REPAIRS
26/4/33-8/5/33**LO** (11)
28/7/34-18/9/34**HG** (45)
29/2/36-17/3/36**HS** (15)
11/1/37-3/2/37**HG** (21)
7/10/37-21/10/37**HS** (13)
4/10/38-11/11/38**HG** (34)
5/12/39-21/12/39**HS** (15)
5/4/41-30/4/41**HG** (22)
25/3/42-28/4/42**LS** (30)
11/8/42-16/9/42**LO** (32)
29/4/43-15/5/43**HS** (15)
13/12/44-3/1/45**HS** (18)
12/11/45-8/12/45**HG** (24)
21/4/47-13/5/47**LS** (20)
6/12/48-2/2/49**HG** (50)
17/4/50-11/5/50**HI** (21)
27/6/50-2/8/50**LC** (31)
25/5/51-24/7/51**LI** (51)
31/7/51-7/8/51**NC(Rect)** (6)
9/10/51-24/11/51**HC (EO)** (40)
11/8/52-11/9/52**LC(EO)** (27)
15/7/53-21/8/53**HI** (32)
3/1/55-31/1/55**HI** (24)
22/6/56-10/8/56**HG** (42)
10/10/57-9/11/57**HI** (26)
9/12/58-14/2/59**HG** (56) AWS GEAR FITTED
30/1/61-15/3/61**LI** (38)
16/3/61-20/3/61**NC(Rect)EO** (3)

### BOILERS

| Fitted | Number | Received From | When Removed Passed To |
|--------|--------|---------------|------------------------|
| 10/4/33 | | | 5533 |
| 22/8/34 | | 5942 | STOCK |
| 9/3/36 | | 5902 | 5509 |
| 19/1/37 | | 5521 | |
| 14/10/37 | 5482 | 5534 | |
| 11/11/38 | 5368 | 6004 | 5503 |
| 30/4/41 | 5369 | 5511 | 5538 |
| 15/5/43 | 6011 | 5535 | 5533 |
| 8/12/45 | 6002 | 5544 | 45513 |
| 2/2/49 | | | |
| 24/11/51 | 6010 | 45515 | 45549 |
| 10/8/56 | 5988 | 45543 | 45507 |
| 14/2/59 | | | |

### MILEAGES

| | |
|----|--------|
| 1933 | 63,481 |
| 1934 | 41,962 |
| 1935 | 61,665 |
| 1936 | 66,099 |
| 1937 | 49,395 |
| 1938 | 54,986 |
| 1939 | 53,135 |
| 1940 | 54,888 |
| 1941 | 45,218 |
| 1942 | 40,473 |
| 1943 | 64,756 |
| 1944 | 39,848 |
| 1945 | 48,978 |
| 1946 | 54,106 |
| 1947 | 46,481 |
| 1948 | 37,547 |
| 1949 | 38,123 |
| 1950 | 37,336 |
| 1951 | 27,234 |
| 1952 | 39,540 |
| 1953 | 41,088 |
| 1954 | 44,656 |
| 1955 | 37,795 |
| 1956 | 38,302 |
| 1957 | 43,272 |
| 1958 | 44,520 |
| 1959 | 41,781 |
| 1960 | 34,992 |

**Mileage at 31/12/50 898,477
Mileage at 31/12/60 1,291,657
Stored 15/11/61 – Withdrawal,
week ending 15/9/62 from Edge
Hill, where, according to the
Record Card, it was 'broken up
1/12/62'. This record probably
doubtful; generally believed to
have been scrapped Crewe
Works 10/62**

45534 E. TOOTAL BROADHURST, the name it got from 5525 in 1937, arriving at Chester General at a truly wonderful moment (there are five locomotives in this view) with the 9.5am Llandudno-Euston on 4 August 1962. Photograph B.W.L. Brooksbank, Initial Photographics.

# 45534 E TOOTAL BROADHURST (from 1937)

Built Derby 25/4/33 Replacement for 5935 (LNWR CLAUGHTON No.713)
*Renumbered 5935 to 5534 13/7/34*
*5534 to 45534 week ending 31/12/48*
*Converted to 6P (later 7P) 31/12/48 (17th of 18)*

## TENDERS

| No | Fitted |
|----|--------|
| 4507 | 25/4/33 |
| | |
| 9765 | 31/12/48 |
| 9037 | 30/4/53 |
| 9781 | 25/9/60 |

## REPAIRS

1/6/34-13/7/34LS (37)
26/3/35-1/5/35HG (31)
30/1/36-6/3/36LS (32)
15/5/36-8/6/36HO (21)
26/1/37-22/2/37HS (24)
12/8/37-1/9/37HG (18)
16/9/38-1/11/38HS (40)
7/7/39-11/8/39HS (31)
7/3/40-3/4/40HG (23)
23/12/40-3/2/41LS (36)
30/6/41-26/7/41HO (24)
25/2/42-28/3/42HS (28)
24/6/43-3/7/43LS (9)
4/8/44-31/8/44HG (24)
14/2/46-15/3/46HS (26)
7/4/46-10/5/46LO (28)
16/9/47-29/10/47LS (38)

4/10/48-31/12/48HG (76)
22/5/50-16/6/50LI (22)
12/7/51-24/8/51LI (37)
11/6/52-7/7/52HI (22)
18/11/52-10/12/52LC(EO) (19)
7/9/53-8/10/53HG (27) SMOKE DEFLECTORS FITTED
29/9/54-3/11/54HI (30)
19/9/55-5/11/55HG (41)
14/11/55-26/11/55NC(Rect)EO (11)
17/9/56-17/10/56LI (26)
13/2/57-8/3/57LC (20)
29/6/57-31/7/57LC(EO) (27)
21/1/58-13/2/58HI (20)
15/12/58-21/1/59HG (30)
7/4/59-24/4/59NC(EO) (15) AWS GEAR FITTED
21/7/60-17/9/60LI (50) SPEEDOMETER FITTED

## BOILERS

| Fitted | Number | Received From | When Removed Passed To |
|--------|--------|---------------|------------------------|
| 25/4/33 | | | 5529 |
| 10/4/35 | | 5505 | STOCK |
| 3/6/36 | | 5506 | |
| 23/8/37 | 5352 | 5551 | 5504 |
| 1/11/38 | 6178 | 5506 | 5527 |
| 3/4/40 | 6012 | 5500 | 5539 |
| 28/3/42 | 5481 | 5512 | 5545 |
| 31/8/44 | 6030 | 5527 | 45518 |
| | | | |
| 31/12/48 | 12674 | NEW | 46142 |
| 8/10/53 | 12673 | 46123 | 46110 |
| 5/11/55 | 13240 | 46100 | 46110 |
| 21/1/59 | 12204 | 46111 | |

## SHEDS

Leeds 25/4/33
Longsight 16/2/35
Leeds 25/7/36
Edge Hill (Loan) 21/8/48
Edge Hill 11/9/48

Crewe North 4/12/48
Bushbury 1/10/49
Longsight 10/6/50
Holyhead (Loan) 15/7/50
Longsight 14/10/50
Camden 11/8/51
Edge Hill 10/11/51
Llandudno Jct 7/11/59
Longsight 18/6/60
Crewe North 10/9/60
Willesden 10/6/61
Llandudno Jct 23/9/61
Crewe North 22/6/63

## MILEAGES

| | |
|------|--------|
| 1933 | 57,198 |
| 1934 | 81,820 |
| 1935 | 70,307 |
| 1936 | 57,092 |
| 1937 | 81,041 |
| 1938 | 76,056 |
| 1939 | 69,738 |
| 1940 | 72,931 |
| 1941 | 60,803 |
| 1942 | 50,317 |
| 1943 | 63,580 |
| 1944 | 36,779 |
| 1945 | 39,940 |
| 1946 | 38,217 |
| 1947 | 36,781 |
| 1948 | 36,340 |
| 1949 | 68,043 |
| 1950 | 58,700 |
| 1951 | 51,841 |
| 1952 | 57,850 |
| 1953 | 64,893 |
| 1954 | 60,181 |
| 1955 | 47,185 |
| 1956 | 57,895 |
| 1957 | 49,017 |
| 1958 | 58,097 |
| 1959 | 60,624 |
| 1960 | 42,056 |

Mileage at 31/12/50 1,055,683
Mileage at 31/12/60 1,605,322
Withdrawn week ending 9/5/64 from Crewe North
Stored 4/11/62-3/2/63, 23/9/63-13/12/63 and 18/1/64-11/3/64
Scrapped Crewe Works 6/64

5535, without name, in early condition (no low rain strip on roof, crosshead-driven vacuum pump) taking water, probably at its home shed, Leeds Holbeck. A classic LMS wheelbarrow in the foreground! 5535's unique feature is the top feed, mentioned in the introductory text, just ahead of the dome fed by a pipe on the right-hand side only. Otherwise the only Patriots with top feed were the rebuilds. Photograph W. Hermiston, The Transport Treasury.

# 45535 SIR HERBERT WALKER K.C.B. (from 1937)

**Built Derby 4/5/33 Replacement for 5997 (LNWR CLAUGHTON No.11)**
*Renumbered 5997 to 5535 11/5/34*
*5535 to 45535 week ending 25/9/48*
*Converted to 6P (later 7P) 25/9/48 (13th of 18)*

### TENDERS

| No | Fitted |
|---|---|
| 4508 | 4/5/33 |
| 9771 | 25/9/48 |

### BOILERS

| Fitted | Number | Received From | When Removed Passed To |
|---|---|---|---|
| 4/5/33 | | | STOCK |
| 25/11/35 | | 5503 | 5519 |
| 31/8/36 | | 5536 | |
| 13/4/38 | 6009 | 6023 | 5547 |
| 13/4/40 | 6011 | 5501 | 5533 |
| 23/9/42 | 6176 | 5549 | 5536 |
| 15/12/45 | 5987 | 5513 | |
| | | | |
| 25/9/48 | 12663 | NEW | 45545 |
| 12/1/52 | 12664 | 45527 | 45522 |
| 29/1/54 | 12204 | 46139 | 46111 |
| 26/7/56 | 13592 | 46140 | 46165 |
| 24/1/59 | 12670 | 46161 | |

### REPAIRS

18/4/34-11/5/34**HS** (21)
9/4/35-1/5/35**LS** (19)
1/11/35-9/12/35**HG** (33)
31/7/36-4/9/36**HS** (31)
10/9/37-22/10/37**LS** (37)
1/4/38-5/5/38**HG** (29)
3/5/39-17/5/39**HS** (13)
25/3/40-13/4/40**HG** (18)
23/9/40-4/10/40**LO** (11)
5/5/41-30/5/41**HS** (23)
9/7/42-23/9/42**HG** (66)
4/2/43-22/2/43**LO** (16)
10/5/43-29/5/43**LO** (18)
11/6/43-20/7/43**LO** (34)
12/1/44-29/1/44**LS** (16)
15/9/44-7/10/44**HS** (20)
28/11/45-15/12/45**HG** (16)
23/1/47-3/3/47**LS** (34)

3/6/48-25/9/48**HG** (99)
12/11/49-29/11/49**LC** (15)
24/4/50-11/5/50**LI** (15)
11/12/50-16/1/51**LC** (30)
3/12/51-12/1/52**HG** (33) SMOKE DEFLECTORS
FITTED
13/4/53-16/5/53**HI** (29)
10/11/53-11/12/53**LC(EO)** (27)
2/1/54-29/1/54**GEN** (23)
26/7/54-24/8/54**LC(EO)** (25)
11/2/55-15/3/55**HI** (27)
14/6/56-26/7/56**HG** (36)
14/12/56-30/1/57**LC(EO)** (38)
5/6/57-29/6/57**LC(EO)** (21)
9/11/57-29/11/57**HI** (17)
29/11/58-24/1/59**HG** (46) AWS GEAR FITTED
23/5/60-17/6/60**LI** (22) SPEEDOMETER FITTED

### SHEDS

Leeds 4/5/33
Longsight 16/2/35
Leeds 25/7/36

Crewe North (loan) 2/10/48
Crewe North 6/11/48
Camden (Loan) 30/9/50
Edge Hill (Loan) 18/11/50
Crewe North 2/12/50
Camden 7/7/51
Crewe North 15/9/51
Edge Hill (Loan) 11/10/52
Crewe North 29/11/52
Edge Hill 12/6/54
Carlisle Kingmoor 3/11/62

### MILEAGES

| 1933 | 64,942 |
|---|---|
| 1934 | 74,317 |
| 1935 | 62,385 |
| 1936 | 80,671 |
| 1937 | 69,059 |
| 1938 | 86,861 |
| 1939 | 78,420 |
| 1940 | 66,846 |
| 1941 | 60,515 |
| 1942 | 47,734 |
| 1943 | 43,211 |
| 1944 | 56,464 |
| 1945 | 45,154 |
| 1946 | 49,639 |
| 1947 | 51,790 |
| 1948 | 46,460 |
| 1949 | 61,361 |
| 1950 | 53,602 |
| 1951 | 53,847 |
| 1952 | 58,945 |
| 1953 | 51,197 |
| 1954 | 50,925 |
| 1955 | 50,427 |
| 1956 | 48,605 |
| 1957 | 51,820 |
| 1958 | 57,873 |
| 1959 | 51,740 |
| 1960 | 51,929 |

Mileage at 31/12/50 1,099,431
Mileage at 31/12/60 1,626,739
Withdrawn week ending 26/10/63
from Carlisle Kingmoor
Scrapped W. Bigley & Sons, Bulwell
9/64

45535 SIR HERBERT WALKER K.C.B. at Crewe (Paint Shop in the background) on 8 April 1962 – note speedo. In terms of maintenance, the inside cylinder of the Patriots was no more of a problem than with any other LM three cylinder engine. All Patriots were used turn and turn about with engines in comparable power classes, so that the originals would be put on whatever class 6 jobs a depot might have and the taper engines on class 7 work. In steam days (there were odd exceptions) power class and not engine type determined the duty. Hence, at Crewe North for instance, class 6 and 7 diagrams were performed by the next Patriot, Rebuilt Patriot, Royal Scot or Jubilee available, according to its power class. By way of an aside, this changed with the coming of the diesels, when separate diagrams were established for different types. Class 47s and the D400s, for example, despite both being Type 4s, had separate diagrams. Photograph F. Hornby, The Transport Treasury.

# 45536 PRIVATE W. WOOD, V.C.

**Built Crewe 4/5/33 Replacement for 6018 (LNWR CLAUGHTON No. 179 PRIVATE W. WOOD, V.C.)**
*Renumbered 6018 to 5536 20/4/34*
*5536 to 45536 week ending 13/11/48*
*Converted to 6P (later 7P) 12/11/48 (16th of 18)*

### TENDERS

| No | Fitted |
|----|--------|
| 4498 | 4/5/33 |
| 4469 | 3/12/38 |
| 4498 | 11/1/39 |
| 9781 | 12/11/48 |
| 9037 | 25/7/60 |

### REPAIRS

6/4/34-20/4/34**LS** (13)
3/9/34-26/9/34**HG** (21)
7/8/35-26/8/35**LS** (17)
30/6/36-30/7/36**HG** (27)
5/1/37-19/1/37**LO** (13)
8/6/37-25/6/37**LS** (16)
11/10/37-12/11/37**HG** (29)
29/10/38-18/11/38**LS** (18)
18/8/39-11/9/39**HG** (21)
5/1/40-26/1/40**LO** (19)
20/1/41-4/2/41**LS** (14)
17/7/42-3/10/42**HG** (68)
26/11/43-16/12/43**HS** (18)
11/1/45-9/2/45**LO** (26)
3/12/45-14/2/46**HG** (63)
20/9/47-22/10/47**HS** (28)
24/10/47-6/11/47**NCRect** (12)
3/2/48-21/2/48**LO** (17)

23/7/48-12/11/48**HG** (97)
3/11/49-10/12/49**LC** (33)
25/7/50-22/8/50**HI** (24)
20/8/51-8/9/51**HI** (17)
24/9/51-5/10/51**NC(Rect)EO** (10)
8/11/52-10/12/52**HG** (27) SMOKE
DEFLECTORS FITTED
18/1/54-12/2/54**LI** (22)
10/5/55-7/7/55**HG** (50)
31/8/56-2/10/56**HI** (27)
6/11/57-7/12/57**HG** (27)
26/1/59-21/2/59**LI** (23) AWS GEAR FITTED
19/10/59-4/12/59**HI** (40)
14/12/60-17/2/61**LI** (54) SPEEDOMETER
FITTED

### BOILERS

| Fitted | Number | Received From | When Removed Passed To |
|--------|--------|---------------|------------------------|
| 4/5/33 | | | 6013 |
| 12/9/34 | | 5532 | STOCK |
| 15/7/36 | | 5993 | |
| 27/10/37 | 5998 | 5501 | 5520 |
| 11/9/39 | 6169 | 5543 | 45511 |
| 3/10/42 | 5979 | 5540 | 45546 |
| 14/2/46 | 6176 | 5535 | 45520 |
| 12/11/48 | 12668 | NEW | 46143 |
| 10/12/52 | 12541 | 45528 | 46123 |
| 7/7/55 | | 12200 | 46154 |
| 7/12/57 | 12669 | 45512 | |

### SHEDS

Longsight 4/5/33
Crewe North 27/11/37
Longsight (Loan) 18/12/37
Crewe North 1/1/38
Longsight (Loan) 15/1/38
Longsight 26/2/38
Crewe North 26/11/38
Longsight 10/12/38
Carlisle Upperby 31/5/41
Preston 4/10/41

Longsight 27/11/48
Bushbury 1/10/49
Longsight 10/6/50
Millhouses 2/60
Canklow 1/62
Darnall 6/62

### MILEAGES

| 1933 | 58,845 |
|------|--------|
| 1934 | 73,404 |
| 1935 | 74,681 |
| 1936 | 78,190 |
| 1937 | 65,768 |
| 1938 | 80,287 |
| 1939 | 67,692 |
| 1940 | 52,586 |
| 1941 | 52,313 |
| 1942 | 31,556 |
| 1943 | 40,368 |
| 1944 | 34,675 |
| 1945 | 30,724 |
| 1946 | 39,405 |
| 1947 | 34,785 |
| 1948 | 37,455 |
| 1949 | 60,871 |
| 1950 | 62,120 |
| 1951 | 59,399 |
| 1952 | 62,685 |
| 1953 | 73,069 |
| 1954 | 61,962 |
| 1955 | 48,889 |
| 1956 | 65,815 |
| 1957 | 62,023 |
| 1958 | 74,983 |
| 1959 | 55,340 |
| 1960 | 46,021 |

**Mileage at 31/12/50 975,725**
**Mileage at 31/12/60 1,585,911**
**Withdrawn week ending 29/12/62**
**from Darnall**
**Scrapped Crewe Works 3/64**

45536 PRIVATE W. WOOD V.C. waiting in the spur at the end of Platform 8/9 at Birmingham New Street, 4 April 1959. The Patriot will take over the northbound Pines Express – in the shadows beyond, BR 4 6 0 73158 is coming off the train. The relatively rare right-facing lion on the second BR crest can be observed. Photograph Michael Mensing.

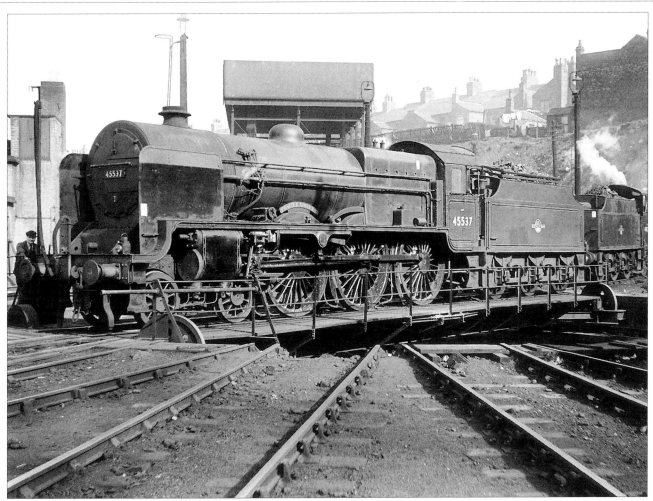

45537 PRIVATE E SYKES V.C., what would seem to be an unusual arrival at Leicester shed on 3 March 1961. In truth it had become not so unusual – 45537 was at Nuneaton by now seeing out its mileage on, among other jobs, the regular pick-up to Leicester. The locomotive might have had only a year or so left to it but Nuneaton kept it commendably clean. Photographs Alec Swain, The Transport Treasury.

# 45537 PRIVATE E. SYKES V.C.

**Built Crewe 19/7/33 Replacement for 6015 (LNWR CLAUGHTON No 158 PRIVATE E. SYKES, V.C.)**
*Renumbered 6015 to 5537 25/6/34*
*5537 to 45537 week ending 8/5/48*

**TENDERS**

| No | Fitted |
|----|--------|
| 4509 | 19/7/33 |
| 4487 | 29/6/54 |
| 3943 | 29/3/58 |
| 3899 | 4/3/60 |

**BOILERS**

| Fitted | Number | Received From | When Removed Passed To |
|--------|--------|---------------|------------------------|
| 19/7/33 | | | 5506 |
| 15/1/36 | | 5535 | STOCK |
| 18/3/37 | 6003 | 5953 | 5540 |
| 29/6/38 | 5984 | 5522 | 5543 |
| 15/7/41 | 5975 | 5508 | 5513 |
| 6/10/45 | 5978 | 5532 | 45547 |
| 11/4/50 | 6172 | 45518 | 45510 |
| 29/11/52 | 5998 | 45549 | 45506 |
| 29/3/58 | 6033 | 45517 | 45513 |
| 4/3/60 | 5994 | 45546 | WDL |

**REPAIRS**

2/6/34-27/6/34HS (22)
26/12/35-28/1/36HG (29)
8/3/37-30/3/37HS (19)
6/6/38-22/7/38HG (41)
1/2/40-15/2/40HS (13)
18/6/41-15/7/41HG (24)
31/1/43-24/2/43LS (21)
1/5/44-17/5/44HS (15)
8/9/45-6/10/45HG (25)
20/2/47-12/4/47LS (44)
17/4/48-7/5/48LS (18)
15/2/49-7/3/49HI (18)
27/2/50-11/4/50HG (36)
2/6/51-22/6/51LI (17)
3/10/52-29/11/52HG (49)
2/12/52-31/12/52NC(Rect)EO (23)
19/1/53-11/2/53LC(EO) (20)
20/4/53-29/5/53LC(EO) (34)
8/6/54-29/6/54LI (18)
23/4/56-30/5/56HI (32)
31/7/56-18/9/56LC(EO) (42)
24/1/58-29/3/58HG (55)
30/5/58-9/7/58NC(Rect)EO (34)
22/10/58-2/12/58HC(EO) (35)
5/12/58-10/12/58NC(EO) (4)
18/1/60-4/3/60HG (40) AWS GEAR FITTED

**SHEDS**

Longsight 29/7/33
Preston 18/7/36
Carlisle Upperby 15/9/51
Preston 5/7/52
Carlisle Upperby 20/9/52
Rugby (Loan) 21/11/59
Rugby 2/1/60
Nuneaton 31/12/60

**MILEAGES**

| | |
|------|--------|
| 1933 | 40,249 |
| 1934 | 78,165 |
| 1935 | 74,413 |
| 1936 | 68,424 |
| 1937 | 56,388 |
| 1938 | 41,773 |
| 1939 | 59,543 |
| 1940 | 53,822 |
| 1941 | 53,265 |
| 1942 | 40,579 |
| 1943 | 42,930 |
| 1944 | 32,236 |
| 1945 | 34,195 |
| 1946 | 41,155 |
| 1947 | 45,499 |
| 1948 | 39,629 |
| 1949 | 48,788 |
| 1950 | 46,178 |
| 1951 | 47,289 |
| 1952 | 30,928 |
| 1953 | 39,175 |
| 1954 | 48,244 |
| 1955 | 34,115 |
| 1956 | 35,795 |
| 1957 | 42,637 |
| 1958 | 23,068 |
| 1959 | 50,360 |
| 1960 | 34,383 |

**Mileage at 31/12/50 897,231**
**Mileage at 31/12/60 1,283,225**
**Withdrawn week ending 9/6/62**
**from Nuneaton**
**Stored 19/11/61 - withdrawal**
**Scrapped Crewe Works 9/62**

5538 (later GIGGLESWICK) in early condition, at Derby on 29 May 1937. It has been in for some valve setting work – note the cleaned up wheels (new tyres probably) and the cryptic chalk markings. Photograph J.A. Whaley, The Transport Treasury.

45538 (it was named GIGGLESWICK in 1938) at Longsight shed on 15 March 1953. Photograph M.N. Bland, The Transport Treasury.

# 45538 GIGGLESWICK (from 4/11/38)

**Built Crewe 21/7/33 Replacement for 6000 (LNWR CLAUGHTON No 15)**
*Renumbered 6000 to 5538 3/8/34*
*5538 to 45538 week ending 26/6/48*

**TENDERS**

| No | Fitted |
|---|---|
| 4510 | 21/7/33 |
| 4558 | 23/8/56 |
| 3909 | 7/10/60 |

**REPAIRS**
10/7/34-3/8/34**LS** (22)
2/4/35-13/5/35**HG** (35)
7/4/36-24/4/36**HS** (15)
18/5/36-29/5/36**LO** (11)
29/3/37-30/5/37**HS** (54)
2/9/37-27/9/37**HG** (22)
25/8/38-21/9/38**HS** (24)
13/6/39-14/8/39**HG** (54)
26/2/40-30/3/40**LO** (29)
25/6/40-12/7/40**LS** (16)
25/9/40-19/10/40**HO** (22)
18/10/41-15/11/41**HS** (25)
29/11/42-2/1/43**LS** (29)
17/11/43-24/12/43**HG** (33)
1/11/44-30/12/44**HS** (51)
13/11/45-1/12/45**LS** (17)
17/12/45-12/1/46**LO** (23)
18/2/47-11/4/47**HG** (45)
26/5/48-22/6/48**LS** (24)
29/6/48-3/7/48**TRO** (5)
10/7/48-24/7/48**TRO** (13)
14/12/49-4/2/50**HG** (44)
21/3/50-21/4/50**LC** (26)
27/5/51-20/6/51**HI** (20)
25/6/51-2/7/51**NC(Rect)** (6)
26/9/52-20/12/52**HG** (73)
19/1/53-9/3/53**LC** (42)
3/6/54-8/7/54**HI** (30)
25/8/55-6/10/55**LI** (36)
9/12/56-26/2/57**HG** (65)
22/8/58-19/9/58**LI** (24)
5/10/59-13/10/59**NC(EO)** (7) AWS
GEAR FITTED
17/8/60-7/10/60**HI** (44)
11/10/60-19/10/60**NC(EO)Rect** (7)
25/10/60-27/10/60**NC(Rect)EO** (2)

**BOILERS**

| Fitted | Number | Received From | When Removed Passed To |
|---|---|---|---|
| 21/7/33 | | | 5509 |
| 23/4/35 | | 6017 | STOCK |
| 20/4/36 | | 5975 | STOCK |
| 10/9/37 | 5989 | 5544 | 5529 |
| 14/8/39 | 5370 | 5515 | 5513 |
| 19/10/40 | 6008 | 5518 | 5543 |
| 24/12/43 | 5369 | 5533 | 5502 |
| 11/4/47 | 6007 | 5530 | 5538 |
| 4/2/50 | 5977 | 5523 | 5504 |
| 20/12/52 | 5984 | 45511 | 45505 |
| 26/2/57 | 5353 | 45502 | WDL |

**SHEDS**
Leeds 21/7/33
Longsight 16/2/35
Leeds 25/7/36
Willesden (Loan) 21/8/48
Willesden 11/9/48
Edge Hill 28/5/49
Preston 22/6/57
Willesden 20/6/59
Nuneaton 14/1/61

**MILEAGES**

| | |
|---|---|
| 1933 | 45,799 |
| 1934 | 73,944 |
| 1935 | 72,382 |
| 1936 | 72,698 |
| 1937 | 65,480 |
| 1938 | 73,679 |
| 1939 | 62,303 |
| 1940 | 59,368 |
| 1941 | 47,304 |
| 1942 | 44,097 |
| 1943 | 51,241 |
| 1944 | 51,790 |
| 1945 | 40,011 |
| 1946 | 46,779 |
| 1947 | 50,649 |
| 1948 | 35,197 |
| 1949 | 34,527 |
| 1950 | 37,086 |
| 1951 | 40,726 |
| 1952 | 35,078 |
| 1953 | 41,734 |
| 1954 | 41,782 |
| 1955 | 43,877 |
| 1956 | 40,457 |
| 1957 | 39,582 |
| 1958 | 39,818 |
| 1959 | 41,917 |
| 1960 | 28,803 |
| 1961 | 20,486 |

**Mileage at 31/12/50 964,334 Final
Mileage 1,378,594
Stored 26/10/61 to withdrawal
Withdrawn week ending 22/9/62
from Nuneaton
Scrapped Crewe Works 11/62**

# 45539 E. C. TRENCH

**Built Crewe 27/7/33 Replacement for 5925 (LNWR CLAUGHTON No 2174 E. C. TRENCH)**
*Renumbered 5925 to 5539 30/6/34*
*5539 to 45539 week ending 24/9/49*

## TENDERS

| No | Fitted |
|---|---|
| 4511 | 27/7/33 |
| 3937 | 18/2/52 |
| 3922 | 5/8/53 |
| 3899 | 4/12/54 |
| 4573 | 1/5/56 (HIGH STRAIGHT SIDED) |
| 4509 | 10/1/57 |

## BOILERS

| Fitted | Number | Received From | When Removed Passed To |
|---|---|---|---|
| 27/7/33 | | | 5548 |
| 7/10/35 | 5975 | 5510 | 5508 |
| 24/6/37 | 5361 | 5975 | 5543 |
| 16/11/38 | 6029 | 5529 | 5529 |
| 16/10/40 | 5996 | 5519 | 5550 |
| 13/6/42 | 6012 | 5534 | 5551 |
| 20/10/43 | 5359 | 5532 | 5551 |
| 25/6/46 | 5358 | 5505 | 45515 |
| 14/3/51 | 5997 | 45516 | |
| 5/8/53 | 5369 | 45546 | 45516 |
| 4/1/58 | 5976 | 45510 | WDL |

## REPAIRS

22/5/34-30/6/34**HO** (35)
18/10/34-15/11/34**HS** (25)
4/6/35-7/6/35**LO** (4)
1/10/35-23/10/35**HG** (20)
12/11/36-4/12/36**LS** (20)
21/6/37-19/7/37**HG** (25)
24/10/38-16/11/38**HS** (21)
15/10/39-1/11/39**LS** (15)
21/9/40-16/10/40**HG** (22)
7/5/42-13/6/42**HS** (33)
6/10/43-20/10/43**HG** (13)
9/1/45-10/2/45**LS** (29)
3/6/46-25/6/46**HG** (20)
12/11/47-6/12/47**LS** (22)
24/8/49-20/9/49**HI** (24)
1/2/51-14/3/51**HG** (35)
15/1/52-18/2/52**HI** (29)
24/6/53-5/8/53**HG** (36)
12/11/54-4/12/54**LI** (19)
22/3/56-1/5/56**HI** (33)
25/11/57-4/1/58**HG** (33)
14/1/59-27/2/59**HI** (38) AWS GEAR FITTED
13/1/60-11/3/60**HC(EO)** (50)

## SHEDS

Preston 19/8/33
Aston 23/9/33
Longsight 7/6/35
Aston 28/9/35
Crewe North 11/3/39
Preston 5/6/48
Crewe North 2/10/48
Longsight 29/4/50
Edge Hill 27/10/56
Willesden 20/6/59
Carnforth 8/10/59
Newton Heath (Loan) 26/3/60
Newton Heath 28/5/60

## MILEAGES

| Year | Mileage |
|---|---|
| 1933 | 29,772 |
| 1934 | 43,918 |
| 1935 | 55,165 |
| 1936 | 55,310 |
| 1937 | 51,278 |
| 1938 | 54,374 |
| 1939 | 49,584 |
| 1940 | 47,094 |
| 1941 | 52,724 |
| 1942 | 46,692 |
| 1943 | 42,019 |
| 1944 | 47,586 |
| 1945 | 53,513 |
| 1946 | 50,334 |
| 1947 | 40,825 |
| 1948 | 41,681 |
| 1949 | 32,313 |
| 1950 | 51,488 |
| 1951 | 45,954 |
| 1952 | 45,226 |
| 1953 | 44,049 |
| 1954 | 45,623 |
| 1955 | 43,734 |
| 1956 | 41,627 |
| 1957 | 36,174 |
| 1958 | 45,071 |
| 1959 | 39,155 |
| 1960 | 31,626 |
| 1961 | 16,835 |

**Mileage at 31/12/50 845,670**
**Lifetime Mileage 1,280,744**
**Withdrawn week ending 16/9/61**
**from Newton Heath**
**Scrapped Crewe Works 10/61**

45539 E.C. TRENCH (named after Ernest Frederick Crosbie Trench, a one-time LNW Chief Engineer) at Willesden on 31 July 1955. Photograph B.K.B. Green, Initial Photographics.

45540 SIR ROBERT TURNBULL with a down Midland Division parcels train at Platform 10, Birmingham New Street, 28 October 1961. The engine hails from Saltley, a rare instance of a Patriot finding its way to the Midland Division late on – though it was not 'returning', for it had started life on the Western Division. The three car Cravens set is probably on a Leicester/Nottingham working. The tender attached to 45540 saw out its time with the original BR emblem. Photograph Michael Mensing.

# 45540 SIR ROBERT TURNBULL

**Built Crewe 7/8/33 Replacement for 5901 (LNWR CLAUGHTON No 116 SIR ROBERT TURNBULL)**
*Renumbered 5901 to 5540 18/7/34*
*5540 to 45540 week ending 22/5/48*
*Converted to 6P (later 7P) 1/11/47 (7ᵗʰ of 18)*

### TENDERS

| No | Fitted |
|----|--------|
| 4512 | 7/8/33 |
| 9758 | 1/11/47 |

### REPAIRS

26/9/34-16/10/34**HS** (18)
6/3/35-11/3/35**LO** (5)
12/12/35-10/1/36**HG** (25)
3/5/37-20/5/37**HS** (16)
23/8/38-29/9/38**HG** (33)
18/9/39-29/9/39**LS** (11)
20/2/41-17/3/41**HG** (22)
10/7/41-15/7/41**LO** (5)
17/2/42-21/2/42**LO** (5)
29/4/42-13/6/42**HS** (40)
28/9/43-20/10/43**HG** (20)
9/10/44-21/10/44**HS** (12)
30/3/45-28/4/45**LO** (26)
24/12/45-12/1/46**LS** (17)
29/8/46-18/10/46**LO** (44)

22/7/47-1/11/47**HG** (89)
8/11/47-14/11/47**NC Rect** (6)
5/5/48-30/5/48**Nil** (14) THIS MAY BE TIME OF REPAINT INTO EXPERIMENTAL LIGHT GREEN: CARD REFERS TO 'NO REPAIR'. SEE ALSO 45531
16/4/49-6/5/49**LI** (18)
11/1/50-6/2/50**LC** (22)
6/9/50-22/9/50**LI** (14)
12/11/51-8/1/52**HG** (46) SMOKE DEFLECTORS FITTED
12/4/53-7/5/53**HI** (21)
22/5/53-11/6/53**NC(EO)** (17)
4/1/54-2/2/54**HI** (25)
20/2/55-15/4/55**HG** (45)
19/3/56-25/4/56**LI** (31)
18/3/57-25/4/57**HG** (32)
21/4/58-16/5/58**HI** (22)
6/1/59-7/2/59**LI** (28) AWS GEAR FITTED
13/10/59-25/11/59**LI** (37)
23/11/60-5/1/61**HI** (45) SPEEDOMETER FITTED
31/7/61-14/9/61**LC(EO)** (39)

### BOILERS

| Fitted | Number | Received From | When Removed Passed To |
|--------|--------|---------------|------------------------|
| 7/8/33 | | | 5547 |
| 23/12/35 | | 5521 | STOCK |
| 11/5/37 | 5369 | 5906 | 5511 |
| 28/9/38 | 6003 | 5537 | 5540 |
| 17/3/41 | 5979 | 5513 | 5536 |
| 13/6/42 | 6170 | 5506 | 5542 |
| 20/10/43 | 6001 | 5519 | 45509 |
| | | | |
| 1/11/47 | 12657 | NEW | 45521 |
| 8/1/52 | 12539 | 45529 | 46135 |
| 15/4/55 | 12675 | 45522 | 45521 |
| 25/4/57 | 11734 | 46117 | |

### SHEDS

Preston 19/8/33
Aston 23/9/33
Crewe North 11/3/39
Edge Hill 29/12/45

Bushbury 8/11/47
Willesden 28/5/49
Bushbury 1/10/49
Longsight 10/6/50
Bushbury 7/11/59
Trafford Park (Loan) 14/1/61
Trafford Park 4/2/61
Saltley 17/6/61
Derby 7/4/62
Carlisle Upperby (Loan) 30/6/62
Carlisle Upperby 21/7/62

### MILEAGES

| Year | Mileage |
|------|---------|
| 1933 | 19,732 |
| 1934 | 47,736 |
| 1935 | 50,944 |
| 1936 | 52,324 |
| 1937 | 49,206 |
| 1938 | 44,222 |
| 1939 | 50,362 |
| 1940 | 46,694 |
| 1941 | 43,881 |
| 1942 | 43,990 |
| 1943 | 47,138 |
| 1944 | 44,825 |
| 1945 | 36,472 |
| 1946 | 45,085 |
| 1947 | 26,952 |
| 1948 | 60,850 |
| 1949 | 60,999 |
| 1950 | 56,967 |
| 1951 | 57,172 |
| 1952 | 73,279 |
| 1953 | 59,250 |
| 1954 | 65,334 |
| 1955 | 54,688 |
| 1956 | 58,554 |
| 1957 | 61,925 |
| 1958 | 62,620 |
| 1959 | 62,108 |
| 1960 | 53,512 |
| 1961 | 24,778 to 31 July |

**Mileage at 31/12/50 828,379 Mileage at 31/12/60 1,436,821**
**Withdrawn week ending 6/4/63 from Carlisle Upperby, still carried 1ˢᵗ BR tender emblem**
**Stored 4/6/62-28/6/62**
**Scrapped Crewe Works 7/63**

Upperby's **45541 DUKE OF SUTHERLAND** (still with LMS on the tender) in post-war LMS lined black works a southbound special milk train on 29 May 1952. The location is the cutting north of Penrith and as usual with Mr Bruton's pictures, there is a wealth of observed detail: the time was 2.12pm on a Thursday and 45541 is running at about 50mph. It looks as though the driver has just closed the regulator, though the limit round the six inches of super-elevation through Penrith was 60mph. Photograph E.D. Bruton.

# 45541 DUKE OF SUTHERLAND

**Built Crewe 15/8/33 Replacement for 5903 (LNWR CLAUGHTON No.21 DUKE OF SUTHERLAND)**
*Renumbered 5903 to 5541 18/5/34*
*5541 to 45541 week ending 1/5/48*

**TENDERS**

| No | Fitted |
|----|--------|
| 4513 | 15/8/33 |
| 4248 | 17/4/50 |
| 4499 | 4/12/52 |
| 4477 | 28/4/54 |
| 4469 | 18/8/55 |
| 3187 | 8/11/58 |
| 4500 | 21/2/59 |

**SHEDS**
Crewe North 19/8/33
Longsight 21/7/34
Camden 14/6/41
Edge Hill 3/1/42
Willesden 23/10/42
Camden 28/4/45
Carlisle Upperby 11/1/47
Preston 11/10/47
Carlisle Upperby 25/10/47
Rugby (Loan) 21/11/59
Rugby 2/1/60
Nuneaton 31/12/60

**REPAIRS**
9/1/34-25/1/34**LO** (15)
20/4/34-18/5/34**LS** (25)
28/1/35-14/2/35**LS** (16)
14/8/35-9/9/35**HG** (23)
22/7/36-10/8/36**HS** (17)
20/11/36-12/1/37**HG** (45)
3/1/38-18/1/38**LS** (14)
11/2/38-26/2/38**LO** (14)
4/1/39-26/1/39**HG** (20)
29/3/40-16/4/40**HS** (16)
29/11/40-13/12/40**LO** (13)
19/5/41-7/6/41**HG** (18)
25/2/42-17/4/42**HS** (45)
13/10/43-13/11/43**LS** (28)
21/3/45-11/4/45**HG** (19)
16/10/46-20/11/46**HS** (31)
11/3/48-26/4/48**HG** (39)
23/3/50-17/4/50**LI** (20)
24/3/51-18/4/51**HI** (21)
6/9/52-4/12/52**HG** (76)
22/3/54-28/4/54**HI** (31)
1/4/55-11/5/55**HI** (33)
12/8/55-18/8/55**LC(TO)** (5)
24/11/56-10/1/57**HG** (38)
1/3/58-29/3/58**LC(EO)** (24)
7/10/58-8/11/58**HG** (28)
20/1/59-21/2/59**LC** (28) AWS
GEAR FITTED
28/3/60-6/5/60**LI** (33)

**BOILERS**

| Fitted | Number | Received From | When Removed Passed To |
|--------|--------|---------------|------------------------|
| 15/8/33 | | | 5519 |
| 23/8/35 | | 5529 | 5504 |
| 29/12/36 | | 5531 | |
| 26/1/39 | 6002 | 5532 | 5544 |
| 7/6/41 | 5479 | 5546 | 5524 |
| 17/4/42 | 6178 | 5527 | 5551 |
| 11/4/45 | 6171 | 5531 | |
| 26/4/48 | 5999 | 5526 | 45544 |
| 4/12/52 | 6012 | 45507 | 45500 |
| 10/1/57 | 6003 | 45508 | 45550 |
| 8/11/58 | 6029 | 45551 | |

**MILEAGES**

| | |
|------|--------|
| 1933 | 29,528 |
| 1934 | 58,928 |
| 1935 | 70,304 |
| 1936 | 74,764 |
| 1937 | 86,665 |
| 1938 | 73,620 |
| 1939 | 61,580 |
| 1940 | 46,749 |
| 1941 | 59,790 |
| 1942 | 38,553 |
| 1943 | 43,475 |
| 1944 | 39,556 |
| 1945 | 36,950 |
| 1946 | 38,361 |
| 1947 | 35,023 |
| 1948 | 31,979 |
| 1949 | 39,244 |
| 1950 | 40,418 |
| 1951 | 38,544 |
| 1952 | 34,123 |
| 1953 | 52,418 |
| 1954 | 45,998 |
| 1955 | 39,673 |
| 1956 | 41,274 |
| 1957 | 47,667 |
| 1958 | 35,414 |
| 1959 | 40,847 |
| 1960 | 29,792 |

**Mileage at 31/12/50 905,487**
**Mileage at 31/12/60 1,311,237**
**Withdrawn week ending 9/6/62**
**from Nuneaton**
**Stored 27/10/61-withdrawal**
**Scrapped Crewe Works 9/62**

**45542 at Crewe North about 1948, it what looks like a form of unlined black. Filled-in crankpin spokes front and back, webbed in centre wheel. Photograph W. Hermiston, The Transport Treasury.**

# 45542

**Built Crewe 13/3/34**
*Renumbered 5542 to 45542 week ending 25/6/49*

**SHEDS**
Kentish Town 24/3/34
Longsight 20/4/35
Crewe North 28/5/35
Longsight 28/9/35
Carlisle Upperby 26/10/40
Patricroft 4/10/41
Crewe North 27/7/46
Carlisle Upperby 5/6/48
Preston 15/11/58
Nuneaton 22/7/61

**REPAIRS**
17/4/35-28/5/35**LS** (35)
13/9/35-11/10/35**HO** (25)
2/3/36-12/3/36**LO** (10)
6/6/36-2/7/36**LS** (23)
14/10/36-18/11/36**HG** (31)
20/9/37-4/10/37**LS** (13)
14/3/38-22/4/38**HG** (34)
27/2/39-29/3/39**LS** (27)
29/1/40-2/3/40**HG** (30)
18/10/40-29/10/40**LO** (10)
29/7/41-15/8/41**LS** (16)
22/9/41-4/10/41**HO** (12)
9/2/42-12/2/42**LO** (4)
6/10/42-7/11/42**HS** (29)
28/10/43-13/11/43**HG** (15)
8/10/45-10/11/45**LS** (30)
1/12/46-19/12/46**HG** (16)
13/2/48-16/3/48**LS** (28)
2/6/49-21/6/49**HI** (17)
17/11/50-3/1/51**HG** (39)
28/9/51-25/10/51**LC(EO)** (23)
6/6/52-3/7/52**HI** (23)
28/12/53-18/1/54**HI** (18)
19/2/54-22/3/54**LC(EO)** (26)
25/4/55-9/6/55**HG** (39)
20/10/55-14/11/55**LC** (21)
21/3/57-29/4/57**HI** (32)
21/5/58-26/6/58**LI** (31)
21/9/59-6/10/59**NC(EO)** (13) AWS
GEAR FITTED
23/1/60-22/3/60**LI** (50)

**TENDERS**

| No | Fitted |
|----|--------|
| 4469 | 13/3/34 |
| 4498 | 13/12/38 |
| 4469 | 11/1/39 |
| 4505 | 30/1/44 |
| 4469 | 22/3/44 |
| 3927 | 9/6/55 |
| 4489 | 19/11/60 |

**BOILERS**

| Fitted | Number | Received From | When Removed Passed To |
|--------|--------|---------------|------------------------|
| 13/3/34 | | | STOCK |
| 28/10/36 | | 5505 | 5525 |
| 31/3/38 | 5357 | 5518 | 5502 |
| 2/3/40 | 5484 | 5946 | |
| 4/10/41 | 5993 | 5544 | 5500 |
| 13/11/43 | 6170 | 5540 | 5542 |
| 19/12/46 | 6175 | 5516 | 45505 |
| 3/1/51 | 6173 | 45512 | 45516 |
| 9/6/55 | 5358 | 45515 | WDL |

**MILEAGES**

| 1934 | 62,028 |
|------|--------|
| 1935 | 57,046 |
| 1936 | 66,003 |
| 1937 | /6,795 |
| 1938 | 80,870 |
| 1939 | 66,537 |
| 1940 | 47,560 |
| 1941 | 36,026 |
| 1942 | 45,005 |
| 1943 | 49,153 |
| 1944 | 42,592 |
| 1945 | 36,699 |
| 1946 | 40,119 |
| 1947 | 48,289 |
| 1948 | 41,825 |
| 1949 | 42,961 |
| 1950 | 35,217 |
| 1951 | 45,193 |
| 1952 | 46,428 |
| 1953 | 38,725 |
| 1954 | 41,957 |
| 1955 | 36,244 |
| 1956 | 44,405 |
| 1957 | 35,606 |
| 1958 | 33,643 |
| 1959 | 33,108 |
| 1960 | 24,699 |

**Mileage at 31/12/50 874,725**
**Mileage at 31/12/60 1,254,733**
**Withdrawn week ending 9/6/62**
**from Nuneaton**
**Stored 27/10/61-withdrawal**
**Scrapped Crewe Works 9/62**

# 45543 HOME GUARD (from 30/7/40)

**Built Crewe 16/3/34**
*Renumbered 5543 to 45543 week ending 28/5/49*

## TENDERS

| No | Fitted |
|----|--------|
| 4470 | 16/3/34 |
| 4471 | 15/12/35 |
| 4479 | 28/6/56 |

## BOILERS

| Fitted | Number | Received From | When Removed Passed To |
|--------|--------|---------------|------------------------|
| 16/3/34 | | | STOCK |
| 25/2/36 | | 6023 | |
| 3/3/37 | 6169 | 5542 | 5536 |
| 2/2/39 | 5361 | 5539 | |
| 5/9/41 | 5984 | 5537 | 5529 |
| 27/4/44 | 6008 | 5538 | 45504 |
| 27/5/49 | 6009 | 45519 | 45547 |
| 26/7/52 | 5988 | 45500 | 45533 |
| 28/6/56 | 6031 | 45519 | 45515 |
| 15/2/58 | 6030 | 45544 | WDL |

## REPAIRS

23/5/35-21/6/35**LS** (25)
9/1/36-9/3/36**HG** (52)
23/10/36-12/11/36**LS** (18)
16/2/37-16/3/37**HO** (25)
18/10/37-9/11/37**HS** (20)
9/1/39-2/2/39**HG** (22)
26/3/40-11/4/40**LS** (15)
11/7/40-27/7/40**LO** (15)
19/8/41-5/9/41**HG** (16)
11/12/42-16/1/43**LS** (31)
2/9/43-18/9/43**HS** (15)
13/4/44-27/4/44**HG** (13)
17/8/45-6/9/45**LS** (18)
9/11/45-8/12/45**LO** (26)
31/3/47-30/4/47**HS** (26)
27/4/49-27/5/49**HG** (27)
25/9/50-20/10/50**LI** (22)
7/5/52-26/7/52**HG** (69)
19/8/52-5/9/52**LC(EO)** (15)
11/5/53-4/6/53**LC(EO)** (21)
25/6/54-3/8/54**HI** (33)
8/5/56-28/6/56**HG** (44)
10/12/57-15/2/58**HG** (56)
15/9/59-17/10/59**HI** (28) AWS GEAR FITTED
26/10/59-6/11/59**NCRect(EO)** (10)

## SHEDS

Kentish Town 24/3/34
Crewe North 16/2/35
Longsight 20/4/35
Crewe North 27/11/37
Camden (Loan) 18/12/37
Crewe North 1/1/38
Longsight (Loan) 12/3/38
Longsight 19/3/38
Carlisle Upperby 23/9/39
Patricroft 4/10/41
Edge Hill 27/7/46
Crewe North 2/10/48
Carlisle Upperby (Loan) 4/10/52
Crewe North 25/10/52
Carlisle Upperby 18/9/54
Preston 15/11/58
Longsight 10/1/59
Edge Hill 31/12/60
Lancaster 5/5/62
Carnforth 2/6/62

## MILEAGES

| Year | Mileage |
|------|---------|
| 1934 | 63,986 |
| 1935 | 69,975 |
| 1936 | 66,290 |
| 1937 | 70,063 |
| 1938 | 72,586 |
| 1939 | 71,418 |
| 1940 | 41,317 |
| 1941 | 37,369 |
| 1942 | 48,704 |
| 1943 | 43,367 |
| 1944 | 58,640 |
| 1945 | 26,972 |
| 1946 | 43,942 |
| 1947 | 40,189 |
| 1948 | 43,813 |
| 1949 | 36,015 |
| 1950 | 42,953 |
| 1951 | 45,211 |
| 1952 | 36,993 |
| 1953 | 44,296 |
| 1954 | 41,364 |
| 1955 | 43,735 |
| 1956 | 45,640 |
| 1957 | 39,589 |
| 1958 | 39,875 |
| 1959 | 38,551 |
| 1960 | 43,576 |

**Mileage at 31/12/50 877,599 Mileage at 31/12/60 1,296,429**
**Withdrawn week ending 17/11/62 from Carnforth**
**Stored 19/1/62-2/5/62, 15/9/62-5/10/62, worked enthusiasts special 14/10/62 and last Patriot job on 16/10/62 and 17/10/62 – withdrawal. In store at Preston MPD as late as 20/7/63 with 45550**
**Scrapped Crewe Works 9/63**

A magnificent HOME GUARD, begrimed and bedraggled but somehow looking in perfect readiness, at Crewe North. There is no date but it had gone to 5A in October 1948 and got the BR number some time later, in May of the following year. So 1949 would be a good bet. Marvellous machines that always made lots of noise, Crewe never hesitated to send these old girls north. A particular problem was always the wrapper type smokebox; this would leak and impair steaming but brick arch cement would come to the rescue – much to the chagrin of the Works staff when they went in for repair. Photograph W. Hermiston, The Transport Treasury.

45543 was never based on the Midland Division and as a Longsight engine it is somewhat surprising to find it at Luton on 1 August 1959, heading 45561 SASKATCHEWAN with a Bradford-St Pancras train. Photograph F. Hornby, The Transport Treasury.

# 45544

**Built Crewe 22/3/34**
*Renumbered 5544 to 45544 week ending 18/9/48*

**TENDERS**

| No | Fitted |
|----|--------|
| 4471 | 22/3/34 |
| 4470 | 15/12/35 |
| 4561 | 6/3/50 |
| 4497 | 3/4/54 |
| 3909 | 2/7/56 |
| 3898 | 17/8/57 |
| 3931 | 5/12/57 |
| 4475 | 1/6/59 |

**REPAIRS**

27/6/35-18/7/35**LS** (19)
7/12/35-13/1/36**HG** (22)
25/11/36-9/12/36**LO** (13)
23/4/37-11/5/37**HS** (16)
27/11/37-10/12/37**LS** (12)
1/2/38-8/3/38**HG** (31)
15/3/39-29/3/39**LO** (13)
11/11/39-27/11/39**HS** (14)
11/6/40-25/6/40**LO** (13)
5/7/41-23/7/41**HG** (16)
5/6/42-23/6/42**LO** (16)
29/9/42-16/10/42**LS** (16)
26/4/44-12/5/44**LS** (15)
27/8/45-15/9/45**HG** (18)
25/4/47-26/5/47**HS** (27)
28/8/48-16/9/48**HS** (17)
29/1/50-6/3/50**HG** (30)
24/7/51-15/8/51**LI** (19)
24/11/52-10/1/53**HG** (39)
9/3/54-3/4/54**HI** (22)
17/5/55-25/6/55**HG** (34)
2/7/56-14/8/56**HI** (37)
30/10/57-5/12/57**HG** (31)
8/1/58-3/2/58**LC** (22)
13/6/58-11/7/58 **LC(EO)** (24)
5/6/59-22/7/59**LI** (43) AWS GEAR FITTED
8/11/60-31/12/60**HG** (44)
10/7/61-5/8/61**LC(EO)** (23)

**SHEDS**

Kentish Town 24/3/34
Carlisle Upperby 16/6/34
Leeds 3/11/34
Crewe North 16/2/35
Longsight 20/4/35
Preston 18/7/36
Patricroft (Loan) 8/12/38
Preston 31/12/38
Crewe North 20/9/52
Edge Hill 29/1/55
Carlisle Upperby 20/6/59
Warrington 10/9/60

**BOILERS**

| Fitted | Number | Received From | When Removed Passed To |
|--------|--------|---------------|------------------------|
| 22/3/34 | | | 5524 |
| 30/12/35 | | 5512 | STOCK |
| 3/5/37 | 5993 | 5502 | STOCK |
| 17/2/38 | 5980 | 5536 | 5545 |
| 23/7/41 | 6002 | 5541 | 5533 |
| 15/9/45 | 5976 | 5530 | 45510 |
| 6/3/50 | 5983 | 6004 | |
| 10/1/53 | 5999 | 45541 | 45508 |
| 25/6/55 | 6030 | 45518 | 45543 |
| 5/12/57 | 6172 | 45518 | |
| 31/12/60 | 6001 | 45510 | WDL |

**MILEAGES**

| 1934 | 55,019 |
|------|--------|
| 1935 | 54,914 |
| 1936 | 77,779 |
| 1937 | 52,352 |
| 1938 | 62,020 |
| 1939 | 52,640 |
| 1940 | 49,805 |
| 1941 | 46,621 |
| 1942 | 41,446 |
| 1943 | 40,552 |
| 1944 | 38,821 |
| 1945 | 33,660 |
| 1946 | 44,910 |
| 1947 | 48,313 |
| 1948 | 46,239 |
| 1949 | 43,089 |
| 1950 | 46,004 |
| 1951 | 42,651 |
| 1952 | 37,328 |
| 1953 | 51,177 |
| 1954 | 43,582 |
| 1955 | 42,348 |
| 1956 | 42,046 |
| 1957 | 42,348 |
| 1958 | 34,408 |
| 1959 | 39,444 |
| 1960 | 30,274 |
| 1961 | 15,695 |

**Mileage at 31/12/50 834,184**
**Lifetime mileage 1,255,485**
**Withdrawn week ending 9/12/61 from Warrington**
**Scrapped Crewe Works 3/62**

Patriot on a branch. Larger power was frequently found on through coaches on the branch from the main line at Oxenholme to Kendal and Windermere. Gleaming in BR green, 45544 has four coaches off the 10.40am Euston-Carlisle express on 4 June 1958. This is nearly five o-clock in the afternoon; the main line is just out of sight by the last tree on the right. Photograph E.D. Bruton.

# 45545 PLANET (from 3/11/48)

**Built Crewe 27/3/34**
*Renumbered 5545 to 45545 week ending 6/11/48*
*Converted to 6P (later 7P) 5/11/48 (15th of 18)*

### TENDERS

| No | Fitted |
|----|--------|
| 4472 | 27/3/34 |
| 3331 | 6/4/48 |
| 9773 | 5/11/48 |

### BOILERS

| Fitted | Number | Received From | When Removed Passed To |
|--------|--------|---------------|------------------------|
| 27/3/34 | | | STOCK |
| 15/6/36 | | 5538 | |
| 27/9/37 | 5976 | 5546 | 5545 |
| 10/10/38 | 5480 | 5519 | 5530 |
| 30/10/39 | 6000 | 5525 | 5505 |
| 4/10/41 | 5980 | 5544 | 5522 |
| 20/12/44 | 5481 | 5534 | 45517 |
| | | | |
| 5/11/48 | 12672 | NEW | 45523 |
| 18/2/52 | 12663 | 45535 | 45528 |
| 14/9/54 | 13239 | 46106 | 46139 |
| 26/2/58 | 12535 | 46100 | |

### REPAIRS

29/4/35-27/5/35**LS** (25)
20/9/35-7/10/35**HO** (15)
5/6/36-30/6/36**HG** (22)
11/12/36-8/1/37**LS** (24)
21/9/37-13/10/37**HG** (20)
8/9/38-10/10/38**HS** (28)
30/10/39-20/11/39**HG** (19)
20/12/40-7/1/41**LS** (15)
10/9/41-4/10/41**HG** (22)
7/6/43-19/6/43**LS** (12)
2/12/44-20/12/44**HG** (16)
19/12/46-11/1/47**LS** (20)

31/7/48-5/11/48**HG** (84)
29/4/50-29/5/50**LI** (25)
2/5/51-29/5/51**LC** (23)
8/1/52-18/2/52**HG** (35) SMOKE
DEFLECTORS FITTED
3/11/52-5/12/52**LC** (28)
6/7/53-11/8/53**HI** (31)
3/8/54-14/9/54**HG** (36)
13/5/55-10/6/55**LC** (24)
3/3/56-4/4/56**HI** (26)
23/12/56-21/1/57**LI** (22)
23/1/58-26/2/58**HG** (29)
16/2/59-14/3/59**LI** (23) AWS GEAR
FITTED
30/8/60-14/10/60**HI** (39)
SPEEDOMETER FITTED
7/4/61-3/5/61**LC(EO)** (31)

### SHEDS

Kentish Town 27/3/34
Carlisle Upperby 16/6/34
Leeds 3/11/34
Crewe North 16/2/35
Longsight 27/5/35
Camden 31/5/41
Willesden 31/1/42
Camden 5/2/44
Willesden 10/11/45
Edge Hill 3/5/47

Longsight 13/11/48
Bushbury 27/11/48
Camden 28/5/49
Crewe North 15/9/56
Camden 23/2/57
Crewe North 4/5/57
Carlisle Upperby 10/6/61

### MILEAGES

| 1934 | 61,354 |
|------|--------|
| 1935 | 60,775 |
| 1936 | 77,723 |
| 1937 | 83,468 |
| 1938 | 81,759 |
| 1939 | 69,343 |
| 1940 | 61,204 |
| 1941 | 70,337 |
| 1942 | 48,303 |
| 1943 | 42,043 |
| 1944 | 46,794 |
| 1945 | 44,578 |
| 1946 | 11,840 |
| 1947 | 39,013 |
| 1948 | 25,574 |
| 1949 | 67,210 |
| 1950 | 71,924 |
| 1951 | 61,146 |
| 1952 | 54,074 |
| 1953 | 69,488 |
| 1954 | 56,425 |
| 1955 | 69,220 |
| 1956 | 62,823 |
| 1957 | 53,952 |
| 1958 | 57,498 |
| 1959 | 55,800 |
| 1960 | 48,800 |

**Mileage at 31/12/50 963,242**
**Mileage at 31/12/60 1,552,468**
**Withdrawn week ending 30/5/64**
**from Carlisle Upperby**
**Scrapped J. Connell, Coatbridge**
**9/64**

5545 (the name PLANET had to await BR days) at Camden shed in original condition. Even to the end of steam, it is unlikely if more powerful yard lamps than these appeared anywhere. These mighty beacons, one each side of the north end of the shed, required their own access gangways; they were in place throughout the 1930s but seem not to have survived the Second World War – during which they could not have been used anyway, because of the blackout. The gangways remained in place to the end of the shed's days. Photograph W. Hermiston, The Transport Treasury.

45545 PLANET on the 2.55pm Liverpool Lime Street-Birmingham New Street at Penkridge, south of Stafford, 13 September 1958. It bore the name from its conversion to 2A taper form at the end of 1948. Photograph Michael Mensing.

# 45546 FLEETWOOD (from 18/7/38)

**Built Crewe 29/3/34**
*Renumbered 5546 to 45546 week ending 8/1/49*

| TENDERS | |
|---|---|
| No | Fitted |
| 4473 | 29/3/34 |
| 4480 | 15/10/54 |

**REPAIRS**
25/2/35-8/3/35**LS** (11)
22/8/35-10/9/35**HO** (17)
17/2/36-2/3/36**LO** (13)
21/7/36-18/8/36**LS** (25)
20/4/37-21/4/37**LO** (2)
28/6/37-30/7/37**HG** (29)
20/5/38-21/5/38**LO** (2)
11/10/38-3/11/38**HS** (21)
9/11/38-22/11/38**LO** (12)
3/1/39-9/2/39**HO** (33)
27/3/40-12/4/40**LS** (15)
2/4/41-2/5/41**HC** (27)
13/7/42-4/8/42**HS** (20)
25/8/43-23/9/43**HG** (26)
9/10/44-25/10/44**HS** (15)
4/1/45-10/2/45**HO** (33)
3/4/46-23/4/46**HG** (17)
8/10/47-22/11/47**LS** (40)
23/11/48-7/1/49**HG** (39)
23/6/50-31/7/50**HI** (32)
31/12/51-27/2/52**HG** (50)
17/12/52-29/1/53**HG** (35)
4/8/54-7/9/54**LI** (29)
11/10/54-5/11/54**LC(EO)** (22)
18/11/54-30/12/54**LC** (34)
18/12/55-20/1/56**HG** (26)
28/5/56-27/6/56**LC** (26)
26/11/57-1/1/58**HI** (29)
2/10/58-13/11/58**HC(EO)** (36)
23/6/59-5/9/59**HG** (64) AWS
**GEAR FITTED**
24/9/60-29/10/60**LC(EO)** (30)

| BOILERS | | | |
|---|---|---|---|
| Fitted | Number | Received From | When Removed Passed To |
| 29/3/34 | | | 5507 |
| 30/8/35 | 5976 | 5509 | 5545 |
| 15/7/37 | 5355 | 5516 | |
| 9/2/39 | 5479 | 5522 | 5541 |
| 2/5/41 | 5353 | 6004 | 5515 |
| 23/9/43 | 5981 | 5521 | 5525 |
| 23/4/46 | 5979 | 5536 | |
| 7/1/49 | 6000 | 45532 | 45520 |
| 27/2/52 | 5369 | 45502 | 45539 |
| 29/1/53 | 5982 | 45547 | 45511 |
| 30/1/56 | 5994 | 45513 | 45537 |
| 5/9/59 | 5977 | 45504 | WDL |

**SHEDS**
Kentish Town 29/3/34
Carlisle Upperby 16/6/34
Leeds 3/11/34
Crewe North 16/2/35
Edge Hill 20/4/35
Newton Heath 8/6/35
Crewe North (Loan) 23/10/42
Crewe North 16/1/43
Willesden 18/11/50
Crewe North 24/11/56
Carlisle Upperby 15/12/56
Crewe North 5/1/57
Warrington 27/6/59
Crewe North 4/7/59
Carnforth 7/11/59
Mold Jct 23/1/60
Warrington 23/4/60

| MILEAGES | |
|---|---|
| 1934 | 51,198 |
| 1935 | 61,086 |
| 1936 | 56,710 |
| 1937 | 56,909 |
| 1938 | 52,027 |
| 1939 | 46,916 |
| 1940 | 42,551 |
| 1941 | 39,312 |
| 1942 | 45,711 |
| 1943 | 41,683 |
| 1944 | 46,812 |
| 1945 | 49,488 |
| 1946 | 47,993 |
| 1947 | 42,760 |
| 1948 | 40,627 |
| 1949 | 42,926 |
| 1950 | 42,922 |
| 1951 | 30,025 |
| 1952 | 36,977 |
| 1953 | 44,424 |
| 1954 | 31,258 |
| 1955 | 45,961 |
| 1956 | 46,037 |
| 1957 | 41,349 |
| 1958 | 41,394 |
| 1959 | 37,337 |
| 1960 | 25,563 |
| 1961 | 24,941 |
| 1962 | - |

**Mileage at 31/12/50 807,631**
**Final mileage 1,212,897**
**Withdrawn week ending 9/6/62**
**from Warrington**
**Stored 5/12/61 to withdrawal**
**Scrapped Crewe Works 8/62**

45546 FLEETWOOD, ex-works from a Heavy General and bright in BR green, on the Saturdays only 1.55pm Euston to Bletchley, 8 March 1952. The location is the bank up to Tring Summit, the train slowing to about 30mph. Photograph E.D. Bruton.

# 45547

**Built Crewe 9/4/34**
*Renumbered 5547 to 45547 week ending 26/2/49*

**TENDERS**

| No | Fitted |
|----|--------|
| 4554 | 9/4/34 |
| 3927 | 7/12/53 |
| 4492 | 28/4/55 |
| 4238 | 17/1/59 |
| 3943 | 27/2/60 |

**REPAIRS**
7/3/35-26/3/35**LS** (17)
14/1/36-12/2/36**HG** (26)
26/4/37-1/6/37**HS** (32)
8/11/37-15/12/37**HG** (33)
2/2/39-4/3/39**LS** (27)
20/6/39-13/7/39**LO** (21)
8/5/40-30/5/40**HG** (20)
21/5/41-12/6/41**LS** (20)
22/10/42-21/11/42**HG** (27)
17/5/44-2/6/44**LS** (15)
17/12/45-22/2/46**HG** (66)
6/6/47-29/7/47**HS** (46)
17/1/49-23/2/49**LI** (33)
6/6/50-23/6/50**HG** (15)
19/10/51-26/11/51**LI** (32)
15/11/52-17/12/52**HC** (27)
7/11/53-7/12/53**HG** (25)
14/12/53-19/12/53**NC(Rect)EO** (5)
27/3/54-24/4/54**LC(EO)** (23)
21/3/55-28/4/55**LI** (32)
24/7/56-29/8/56**HI** (31)
9/12/57-11/1/58**HG** (27)
11/1/60-27/2/60**LI** (41) AWS GEAR FITTED
15/10/60-12/11/60**LC(EO)** (24)
11/3/61-1/5/61**HG** (42)

**BOILERS**

| Fitted | Number | Received From | When Removed Passed To |
|--------|--------|---------------|------------------------|
| 9/4/34 | | | 5514 |
| 30/1/36 | | 5540 | STOCK |
| 30/11/37 | 5987 | 5517 | 5511 |
| 30/5/40 | 6009 | 5535 | 5519 |
| 21/11/42 | 6005 | 5514 | |
| 22/2/45 | 5982 | 5549 | 45546 |
| 23/6/50 | 5978 | 5537 | 45550 |
| 7/12/53 | 6009 | 45543 | 45517 |
| 11/1/58 | 6175 | 45524 | |
| 1/5/61 | 5999 | 45508 | WDL |

**SHEDS**
Preston 28/4/34
Newton Heath 11/8/34
Crewe North (Loan) 5/12/42
Crewe North 16/1/43
Edge Hill (Loan) 23/1/43
Edge Hill 27/2/43
Crewe North 2/10/48
Preston (Loan) 19/8/50
Crewe North 14/10/50
Edge Hill (Loan) 11/11/50
Crewe North 6/1/51
Willesden 29/1/55
Carnforth 3/10/59
Willesden 17/10/59
Llandudno Jct 7/1/61
Edge Hill 10/6/61

**MILEAGES**

| 1934 | 63,396 |
|------|--------|
| 1935 | 79,466 |
| 1936 | 60,791 |
| 1937 | 45,974 |
| 1938 | 63,864 |
| 1939 | 39,465 |
| 1940 | 43,427 |
| 1941 | 41,442 |
| 1942 | 39,751 |
| 1943 | 41,551 |
| 1944 | 36,097 |
| 1945 | 39,000 estimated* |
| 1946 | 43,397 |
| 1947 | 38,068 |
| 1948 | 53,239 |
| 1949 | 42,776 |
| 1950 | 49,066 |
| 1951 | 39,934 |
| 1952 | 44,447 |
| 1953 | 40,593 |
| 1954 | 41,261 |
| 1955 | 33,218 |
| 1956 | 36,311 |
| 1957 | 36,616 |
| 1958 | 41,431 |
| 1959 | 40,183 |
| 1960 | 31,957 |

**Mileage at 31/12/50 820,770**
**Mileage at 31/12/60 1,206,000 approx\***
**Withdrawn week ending 15/9/62 from Edge Hill**
**Stored 11/11/61-withdrawal.**
**Had HG repair/boiler change 1/5/61.**
**Scrapped Crewe Works 11/62**

**45547 at Willesden, then its home shed, 17 January 1960. The tender still carries the old BR emblem, though this would have gone with one of the last (the last?) Patriot Heavy Generals, in mid-1961. After that the engine saw out its days working from Edge Hill. Photograph Peter Groom.**

# 45548 LYTHAM ST ANNES (from 18/12/37)

**Built Crewe 27/4/34**
*Renumbered 5548 to 45548 week ending 2/4/49*

**TENDERS**

| No | Fitted |
|----|--------|
| 4555 | 27/4/34 |

**BOILERS**

| Fitted | Number | Received From | When Removed Passed To |
|--------|--------|---------------|------------------------|
| 27/4/34 | | | 5521 |
| 25/10/35 | | 5539 | STOCK |
| 12/11/37 | 6001 | 5526 | 5519 |
| 4/6/40 | 5977 | 5502 | 5523 |
| 6/9/44 | 6174 | 5529 | |
| 29/3/49 | 6032 | 5524 | 45551 |
| 13/8/52 | 6002 | 45513 | 45550 |
| 13/9/56 | 5975 | 45517 | WDL |

**REPAIRS**
12/1/35-1/2/35**LS** (18)
5/8/35-9/8/35**LO** (5)
9/10/35-12/11/35**HG** (20)
25/1/37-22/2/37**LS** (25)
1/11/37-30/11/37**HG** (26)
9/3/39-14/4/39**LS** (31)
17/5/40-4/6/40**HG** (16)
30/6/41-26/7/41**LS** (24)
23/11/42-26/12/42**LS** (29)
19/8/44-6/9/44**HG** (16)
2/2/46-20/2/46**HS** (16)
11/8/47-11/9/47**LS** (28)
28/1/49-29/3/49**HG** (52)
8/11/50-29/11/50**LI** (18)
1/7/52-13/8/52**HG** (37)
25/3/53-31/3/53**NC(EO)** (5)
24/3/54-14/5/54**HI** (43)
21/7/56-13/9/56**HG** (46)
7/6/57-4/7/57**LC** (23)
16/10/58-22/11/58**HI** (32)
25/4/60-4/5/60**NC(EO)** (9) AWS
GEAR FITTED
6/8/60-30/9/60**HI** (47)
5/10/60-14/10/60**NCRectEO** (8)

**SHEDS**
Preston 28/4/34
Newton Heath 11/8/34
Crewe North (Loan) 2/1/43
Crewe North 16/1/43
Carnforth 7/11/59
Rugby 23/4/60
Nuneaton 31/12/60

**MILEAGES**

| 1934 | 61,326 |
|------|--------|
| 1935 | 74,372 |
| 1936 | 63,869 |
| 1937 | 47,718 |
| 1938 | 61,651 |
| 1939 | 46,632 |
| 1940 | 44,236 |
| 1941 | 42,741 |
| 1942 | 40,561 |
| 1943 | 44,703 |
| 1944 | 44,385 |
| 1945 | 44,987 |
| 1946 | 46,601 |
| 1947 | 36,996 |
| 1948 | 46,171 |
| 1949 | 37,584 |
| 1950 | 40,695 |
| 1951 | 39,693 |
| 1952 | 40,223 |
| 1953 | 46,542 |
| 1954 | 42,704 |
| 1955 | 44,671 |
| 1956 | 30,445 |
| 1957 | 43,344 |
| 1958 | 38,421 |
| 1959 | 46,613 |
| 1960 | 22,837 |
| 1961 | 22,809 |
| 1962 | Nil |

**Mileage at 31/12/50 825,228**
**Final Mileage 1,243,530**
**Withdrawn week ending 9/6/62**
**from Nuneaton**
**Stored 1/11/61 to withdrawal**
**Scrapped Crewe Works 10/62**

45548 LYTHAM ST ANNES with the 12.15pm ex-Blackpool North, after arrival at Birmingham New Street Platform 3, 19 September 1959. Photograph Michael Mensing.

Out of the way sighting of a Patriot – Crewe North's 5549, elevating the term 'begrimed' to unseen heights, awaits a job home at Stranraer shed of all places, on 23 April 1948. They would not have a common sight there, you have to think. Renumbering did not come till the following year. Photograph H.C. Casserley.

# 45549

Built Crewe 27/4/34
*Renumbered 5549 to 45549 week ending 12/2/49*

**TENDERS**

| No | Fitted |
|---|---|
| 4556 | 27/4/34 |

**REPAIRS**

28/9/34-14/11/34**LO** (41)
29/4/35-1/6/35**LS** (30)
16/6/36-17/7/36**HG** (28)
21/6/37-14/7/37**LS** (21)
13/4/38-13/5/38**HG** (27)
1/3/39-22/3/39**LO** (19)
31/5/39-1/7/39**HS** (26)
17/4/40-9/5/40**LS** (20)
2/10/40-10/1/41**HO** (86)
23/5/41-20/6/41**LS** (25)
28/9/41-7/10/41**LO** (8)
26/6/42-14/8/42**HG** (43)
8/2/44-25/2/44**HS** (16)
22/3/45-11/5/45**HS** (43)
11/6/45-12/7/45**LO** (28)
22/11/45-8/1/46**HG** (40)
22/9/47-23/10/47**LS** (28)
22/12/48-12/2/49**HG** (45)
17/9/49-15/10/49**LC** (25)
22/10/49-28/10/49**NC(Rect)** (6)
18/11/50-11/12/50**HI** (19)
15/7/52-17/9/52**HG** (55)
1/10/52-15/10/52**LC(EO)** (12)
11/1/54-5/2/54**HI** (22)
28/5/55-25/6/55**HI** (24)
11/8/56-5/10/56**HG** (47)
10/10/56-16/10/56**NC(Rect)(EO)** (5)
9/8/57-31/8/57**LC(EO)** (19)
26/6/58-9/8/58**LI** (38)
23/8/59-6/10/59**NC(EO)** (37) AWS GEAR FITTED
20/5/60-6/7/60**HG** (40)
21/8/61-25/10/61**LC(EO)** (56)

**BOILERS**

| Fitted | Number | Received From | When Removed Passed To |
|---|---|---|---|
| 27/4/34 | | | 5549 |
| 9/7/36 | | | 5549 |
| 14/8/42 | 5982 | 5523 | 5547 |
| 8/1/46 | 6011 | 5533 | |
| 12/2/49 | 5998 | 45505 | 45537 |
| 17/9/52 | 5986 | 45524 | 45508 |
| 5/10/56 | 6010 | 45533 | 45515 |
| 6/7/60 | 6002 | 45550 | WDL |

**SHEDS**

Polmadie 27/4/34
Crewe North (Loan) 18/1/41
Crewe North 1/2/41
Willesden 28/8/48
Longsight 28/5/49
Crewe North 18/6/49
Carlisle Upperby 29/4/50
Edge Hill 15/11/58
Carlisle Upperby 20/6/59
Warrington 23/4/60

**MILEAGES**

| | |
|---|---|
| 1934 | 48,376 |
| 1935 | 78,624 |
| 1936 | 62,833 |
| 1937 | 54,334 |
| 1938 | 62,406 |
| 1939 | 36,250 |
| 1940 | 33,226 |
| 1941 | 43,809 |
| 1942 | 38,429 |
| 1943 | 45,545 |
| 1944 | 44,968 |
| 1945 | 34,431 |
| 1946 | 53,320 |
| 1947 | 36,188 |
| 1948 | 38,848 |
| 1949 | 33,900 |
| 1950 | 37,768 |
| 1951 | 46,850 |
| 1952 | 32,071 |
| 1953 | 41,268 |
| 1954 | 40,904 |
| 1955 | 40,595 |
| 1956 | 38,222 |
| 1957 | 42,116 |
| 1958 | 35,896 |
| 1959 | 38,271 |
| 1960 | 27,316 |

**Mileage at 31/12/50 783,255 Mileage at 31/12/60 1,166,764**
**Withdrawn week ending 16/6/62 from Warrington**
**To store 19/11/61 until withdrawal**
**Scrapped Crewe Works 8/62**

A justly famous image, BR lined black 45549 passing the platelayers' hut at the entrance to the Summit cutting at Shap, banked by 2-6-4T 42403, 6 June 1952. The train is the Class 'D' Liverpool-Carlisle with a minimum of one third of the wagons vacuum fitted. Photograph E.D. Bruton.

# 45550

**Built Crewe 1/5/34**
*Renumbered 5550 to 45550 week ending 22/10/49*

## TENDERS

| No | Fitted |
|---|---|
| 4557 | 1/5/34 |
| 4573 | 29/12/42 (HIGH STRAIGHT SIDED) |
| 4242 | 23/1/56 |
| 4558 | 31/7/56 |
| 4510 | 23/8/56 |
| 4475 | 3/5/58 |
| 3931 | 1/6/59 |

## REPAIRS

24/1/35-14/2/35**LS** (19)
5/3/36-11/4/36**LS** (33)
10/2/37-10/3/37**HS** (25)
6/9/37-6/11/37**HS** (54)
14/10/38-8/11/38**LS** (22)
26/7/39-26/8/39**HG** (28)
7/10/39-26/10/39**LO** (17)
23/9/40-18/10/40**LS** (23)
6/8/41-22/8/41**LS** (15)
3/7/42-4/9/42**HG** (55)
2/12/42-29/12/42**LO** (23)
20/9/43-9/10/43**HS** (18)
18/10/43-23/10/43**LO** (6)
17/10/44-4/11/44**HS** (17)
1/1/45-2/2/45**TRO** (29)
23/5/46-11/6/46**HG** (17)
24/1/48-26/2/48**LS** (29)
29/8/49-21/10/49**HG** (47)
16/4/51-5/5/51**LI** (17)
16/8/52-8/11/52**HG** (72)
12/11/52-6/12/52**NC(Rect)EO** (21)
5/12/53-1/1/54**HI** (21)
18/6/55-30/7/55**HI** (36)
23/1/56-23/1/56**NC(TO)** (1)
16/8/56-20/10/56**HG** (56)
30/10/56-10/11/56**NC(Rect)EO** (10)
4/9/57-4/10/57**LC** (26)
5/4/58-3/5/58**HI** (24)
24/11/59-16/1/60**HG** (44) AWS GEAR FITTED
2/3/61-27/4/61**LC(EO)** (47)
28/8/61-2/11/61**HI** (57)

## BOILERS

| Fitted | Number | Received From | When Removed Passed To |
|---|---|---|---|
| 1/5/34 | | | 5550 |
| 19/2/37 | | 5550 | |
| 26/8/39 | 6033 | 'CREWE' | 5502 |
| 4/9/42 | 5996 | 5539 | 5504 |
| 11/6/46 | 6005 | 5547 | 45508 |
| 21/10/49 | | | |
| 8/11/52 | 6176 | 45520 | 45501 |
| 20/10/56 | 6002 | 45548 | 45549 |
| 16/1/60 | 6003 | 45541 | WDL |

## SHEDS

Preston 5/5/34
Polmadie 6/7/34
Crewe North (Loan) 7/12/40
Preston (Loan) 11/1/41
Preston 1/2/41
Patricroft 6/6/42
Carlisle Upperby 27/7/46
Preston 13/6/53
Edge Hill 19/9/53
Carlisle Upperby 20/6/59
Aston 18/6/60
Warrington 5/8/61
Lancaster 5/5/62
Carnforth 2/6/62

## MILEAGES

| 1934 | 56,447 |
|---|---|
| 1935 | 72,514 |
| 1936 | 73,243 |
| 1937 | 51,371 |
| 1938 | 59,295 |
| 1939 | 53,704 |
| 1940 | 49,889 |
| 1941 | 42,787 |
| 1942 | 37,491 |
| 1943 | 40,158 |
| 1944 | 48,290 |
| 1945 | 39,817 |
| 1946 | 34,510 |
| 1947 | 42,537 |
| 1948 | 37,102 |
| 1949 | 32,283 |
| 1950 | 47,844 |
| 1951 | 45,014 |
| 1952 | 30,249 |
| 1953 | 45,348 |
| 1954 | 45,560 |
| 1955 | 37,661 |
| 1956 | 35,712 |
| 1957 | 44,663 |
| 1958 | 44,288 |
| 1959 | 31,410 |
| 1960 | 34,775 |
| 1961 | 18,940 to 28/8/61 |

Heavy intermediate repair, ex works 2/11/61
**To store 15/11/61 to 2/5/62, 15/9/62 to withdrawal - still in store at Preston MPD as late as 20/7/63 with 45543**
Mileage at 31/12/50 819,282 Mileage at 31/12/60 1,213,962
**Withdrawn week ending 1/12/62 from Carnforth - last of original class to be withdrawn from service Scrapped Crewe Works 8/63**

**45550 at Shrewsbury, doubtless running in from Crewe. It carried this high sided tender from 1942 to 1956 and was at Upperby (then 12A) from 1946 to 1953, followed by six years at Preston. Photograph Paul Chancellor Collection.**

45550 at Willesden shed, 18 June 1960, now with flush riveted tender and AWS. The painted-on shed code 3D refers to Aston – the transfer took place officially this very day, so someone got in quickly, overlooking that the '3' series of Birmingham sheds were, or would be, swallowed up in the mighty Saltley '21' series that very month. Photograph Peter Groom, having climbed into a stores wagon by the look of it.

The final Patriot, 5551, leaving for the south, with fifteen coaches at Crewe in the 1930s. In the background is the Carriage Shed.

# 45551

**Built Crewe 2/5/34**
*Renumbered 5551 to 45551 week ending 29/5/48*

## TENDERS

| No | Fitted |
|----|--------|
| 4558 | 2/5/34 |
| 4560 | 20/9/34 |
| 4558 | 4/10/34 |
| 4242 | 31/7/56 |
| 4570 | 2/5/58 (HIGH STRAIGHT SIDED) |

## BOILERS

| Fitted | Number | Received From | When Removed Passed To |
|--------|--------|--------------|------------------------|
| 2/5/34 | | | 5504 |
| 26/7/35 | | 6004 | STOCK |
| 26/4/37 | | 5520 | |
| 15/8/38 | 5483 | 5524 | 5508 |
| 13/11/40 | 5356 | 5512 | 5551 |
| 15/8/42 | 5356 | 5551 | |
| 3/1/44 | 6012 | 5539 | 5507 |
| 15/9/45 | 6178 | 5541 | |
| 5/6/47 | 5359 | 5539 | |
| 23/11/49 | 6003 | 45517 | 45508 |
| 1/11/52 | 6032 | 45548 | 45509 |
| 26/9/56 | 6029 | 45510 | 45541 |
| 2/5/58 | 6173 | 45516 | WDL |

## REPAIRS

27/10/34-16/11/34**LS** (18)
18/7/35-5/8/35**HS** (16)
22/5/36-5/6/36**LS** (13)
14/4/37-10/5/37**HG** (23)
30/12/37-25/1/38**LS** (23)
18/7/38-15/8/38**HS** (25)
23/11/39-20/12/39**HS** (24)
23/9/40-13/11/40**HG**(45)
17/7/42-15/8/42**HS** (26)
25/8/42-14/9/42**LO** (18)
13/12/43-3/1/44**HG** (18)
21/8/44-2/9/44**LO** (12)
27/8/45-15/9/45**HS** (18)
5/5/47-5/6/47**HG** (28)
16/4/48-24/5/48**LO** (33)
30/12/48-31/1/49**LI** (28)
30/9/49-23/11/49**HG** (47)
15/5/51-6/6/51**LI** (19)
25/8/52-1/11/52**HG** (59)
4/11/52-8/11/52**NC(Rect)EO** (4)
20/8/54-21/9/54**HI** (27)
28/9/55-28/10/55**HI** (26)
13/7/56-26/9/56**HG** (56)
12/3/58-2/5/58**HG** (43)
6/5/58-12/5/58**NC(Rect)EO** (5)
5/6/58-17/6/58**NC(Rect)EO** (10)
7/9/59-23/10/59**HI** (40) SHEET/CARD
MISSING. POSSIBLE AWS GEAR FITTED

## SHEDS

Preston 5/5/34
Camden 23/6/34
Willesden 10/6/39
Crewe North 22/3/41
Carlisle Upperby 14/1/50
Camden 25/6/60
Willesden 9/7/60
Edge Hill 10/6/61

## MILEAGES

| Year | Mileage |
|------|---------|
| 1934 | 41,240 |
| 1935 | 77,164 |
| 1936 | 76,120 |
| 1937 | 71,812 |
| 1938 | 71,557 |
| 1939 | 58,003 |
| 1940 | 43,111 |
| 1941 | 50,632 |
| 1942 | 43,066 |
| 1943 | 49,365 |
| 1944 | 48,325 |
| 1945 | 44,203 |
| 1946 | 44,419 |
| 1947 | 44,418 |
| 1948 | 39,033 |
| 1949 | 36,491 |
| 1950 | 45,473 |
| 1951 | 44,516 |
| 1952 | 24,558 |
| 1953 | 45,959 |
| 1954 | 38,231 |
| 1955 | 42,914 |
| 1956 | 41,232 |
| 1957 | 45,271 |
| 1958 | 38,330 |
| 1959 | 38,773 |
| 1960 | 45,916 |

**Mileage at 31/12/50 884,432**
**Mileage at 31/12/60 1,290,132**
**Withdrawn week ending 16/6/62**
**from Edge Hill**
**Stored 16/11/61-withdrawal**
**Scrapped Crewe Works 10/62**

Last look at a high sided tender; in its last months as a Carlisle Upperby engine, before finishing its days at Camden, Willesden and Edge Hill, 45551 finds itself at Polmadie on 4 June 1960. Photograph J.L. Stevenson, courtesy Hamish Stevenson.

# Dates of Scapping

45500    Crewe Works 4.61
45501    Crewe Works 9.61
45502    Crewe Works 10.60
45503    Crewe Works 9.61
45504    Crewe Works 3.62
45505    Crewe Works 8.62
45506    Crewe Works 3.62
45507    Horwich Works 3.63
45508    Crewe Works 12.60
45509    Crewe Works 9.61
45510    Crewe Works 8.62
45511    Crewe Works 3.61
45512    Motherwell Machinery & Scrap Co. Wishaw 7.65
45513    Crewe Works 10.62
45514    Crewe Works 6.61
45515    Crewe Works 8.62
45516    Crewe Works 9.61
45517    Crewe Works 7.62
45518    Horwich Works 2.63
45519    Crewe Works 3.62
45520    Crewe Works 6.62
45521    Crewe Works 11.63
45522    Central Wagon Co. Ince, Wigan 6.65
45523    Crewe Works 3.64
45524    Crewe Works 10.62
45525    Crewe Works 6.63
45526    T.W.Ward, Coatbridge 1.65
45527    West Of Scotland Shipbreaking Co. Troon 2.65
45528    Crewe Works 3.63
45529    Crewe Works 3.64
45530    Motherwell Machinery & Scrap Co. Wishaw 3.66
45531    G.H.Campbell & Co., Airdrie 1.66
45532    G.H.Campbell & Co., Airdrie 12.64
45533    Crewe Works 10.62
45534    Crewe Works 6.64
45535    W.Bigley & Sons, Bulwell 9.64
45536    Crewe Works 3.64
45537    Crewe Works 9.62
45538    Crewe Works 11.62
45539    Crewe Works 10.61
45540    Crewe Works 7.63
45541    Crewe Works 9.62
45542    Crewe Works 9.62
45543    Crewe Works 9.63
45544    Crewe Works 3.62
45545    J.Connell, Coatbridge 9.64
45546    Crewe Works 8.62
45547    Crewe Works 11.62
45548    Crewe Works 10.62
45549    Crewe Works 8.62
45550    Crewe Works 8.63
45551    Crewe Works 10.62